KU-110-158

CITYPACK
Tokyo

By Martin Gostelow

Fodor's

Fodor's Travel Publications, Inc.
New York • Toronto • London • Sydney • Auckland

HTTP://WWW.FODORS.COM/

Contents

Life 5 – 12

How to organize your time 13 – 24

Top 25 sights 25 – 50

About this book

KEY TO SYMBOLS

✚ map reference on the fold-out
map accompanying this book
(see below)

✉ address

☎ telephone number

🕐 opening times

🍴 restaurant or café on premises
or nearby

Ⓜ nearest subway station

🚃 nearest train station

🚌 nearest bus route

⛴ nearest riverboat or ferry stop

♿ facilities for visitors with
disabilities

✋ admission charge

↔ other nearby places of interest

❓ tours, lectures, or special events

➤ cross-reference (see below)

ℹ tourist information

ORGANIZATION

Citypack Tokyo's six sections cover the six most important aspects of your visit to
Tokyo:

- Tokyo life—the city and its people
- Itineraries, walks, and excursions—how to organize your time
- The top 25 sights, numbered 1–25 from west to east across the city
- Features about different aspects of the city that make it special
- Detailed listings of restaurants, hotels, shops, and nightlife
- Practical information

In addition, text boxes provide fascinating extra facts and snippets, highlights of
places to visit, and invaluable practical advice.

CROSS-REFERENCES

To help you make the most of your visit, cross-references, indicated by ➤ , show
you where to find additional information about a place or subject.

MAPS

- **The fold-out map** in the wallet at the back of the book is a comprehensive
street plan of Tokyo. All the map references given in the book refer to this map.
For example, the Japanese Sword Museum in Yoyogi, Shibuya-ku, has the
following information: ✚ C5—indicating the grid square of the map in which
the Japanese Sword Museum will be found.
- **The city-center maps** found on the inside front and back covers of the book
itself are for quick reference. They show the Top 25 Sights, described on pages
26–50, which are clearly plotted by number (**1** – **25**, not page number) from west
to east.

PRICES

Where appropriate, an indication of the cost of an establishment is given by **$**
signs: **$$$** denotes higher prices, **$$** denotes average prices, while **$** denotes
lower charges.

TOKYO *life*

INTRODUCING TOKYO

Salaryman

He's the man in the dark suit and white shirt, seen on the subway or hurrying to the office, where he'll work until 7PM and then go to a bar to unwind, still with the people he's been with all day. They will drink, smoke, and snack, and may not get home until after midnight. Salaryman joined the company straight from college and hopes to spend his career climbing the corporate ladder, although the old idea of a job for life is fading fast.

A Japanese tradition, the tea ceremony

At first sight, the urban sprawl looks discouragingly gray and monotonous, but don't be put off. As you begin to bring the city into focus, you see it as self-contained districts that are like separate towns and villages, each with its own flavor. The superb subway system puts them within minutes of each other.

Tokyo offers few architectural delights. Buildings are supposed to withstand earthquakes of 7.5 on the Richter scale (although the 1995 Kobe disaster threw such standards into doubt), and perhaps you can't expect beauty as well. The pleasures are all the greater when you discover them: an exquisite art collection on the top floor of an anonymous office tower; a tranquil shrine in the shadow of an elevated expressway. Even in the heart of the hectic city you are aware of the seasons: winter's frosts, spring blossom in the parks and gardens, summer's oppressive humidity, the gold of autumn leaves.

People take care of their own space, and the infinitely courteous local police look after their own little neighborhoods, on foot or bicycle or on duty in a roadside hut. Street crime and petty theft are almost unknown. The chief danger is getting lost, but someone will always be there to help put you right. Huge numbers are constantly on the move but the crowds are managed with remarkable efficiency. In any other country there would be bad temper and bedlam. Here, patience and self-control are instilled from birth and reinforced by example. As a *gaijin*, a foreigner, you will stand out among the least mixed population of any great city.

Shinjuku at night

For one thing, you may not be as impeccably dressed. Judging by the shoppers in Ginza or the boutiques of Omotesando-dori, Tokyo is the fashion capital of the world, although most modern young women still wear a kimono on special occasions, even if mother or grandmother must demonstrate how to put it on.

Night transforms Tokyo, disguising ugly buildings with rainbows of light. Ten thousand restaurants and drinking dens beckon with flashing signs and glowing lanterns. In spite of years of recession and worries about job security, there still seems to be money to spend on leisure. It's important to be part of the group, and office workers like to let off steam together after the long day. A few beers or whiskies soon put them in the mood. Salaryman and boss may compete to sing songs in a karaoke bar, or even talk frankly to each other. Toward midnight, the streets in the entertainment districts are full of cheerfully intoxicated revelers heading for the last train home to sleep it off before the battle to get to work begins again.

Oeru

A woman is still not expected to have a career. To fill in the years until she gets married, she might work as an "office lady" or OL, pronounced "o-eru." Men take the "real" jobs: she shuffles paper, pours tea, and looks pretty. But the *oeru* exacts a sort of revenge: a young salaryman has to spend his spare money socializing with colleagues, while, in spite of her lower pay, she can afford to take foreign vacations. Her horizons may become so wide that he seems gauche and inexperienced.

7

TOKYO IN FIGURES

GEOGRAPHY

- Latitude 35° 41' N, longitude 139° 41' E. Tokyo is farther south than Sicily, level with central California
- Altitude: sea level to 200 feet
- Distance from New York: 6,200 miles
- Distance from London: 6,725 miles
- Distance from Berlin: 5,640 miles
- Distance from Sydney: 4,850 miles
- Area: 783 sq. mi. The inner metropolitan area (226 sq. mi.) is made up of 23 wards, some of them big cities in their own right
- Population of the inner metropolitan area: 8,500,000; of the greater metropolitan area: 12,500,000

FINANCE

- Annual budget of the Tokyo prefecture government: ¥7,000,000,000,000 ($50 billion, £30 billion)
- Property values range up to $100,000 per square yard

PEOPLE

- Five million people travel to work
- An hour's ride to work is typical, two hours not unusual; at least half of all commuters appear to be asleep
- Of 5 million motor vehicles in the city, 2 million are in use on any given day
- Tokyo's citizens watch an average of 26 hours TV per week
- The main extracurricular activity for schoolchildren is extra classes
- Literacy: 99.7 percent
- Life expectancy is among the world's highest: 83 for women; 76 for men
- There are more restaurants per capita than anywhere in the world, even the USA
- 75 percent of men say they get drunk at least one night a week

WORRIED TOKYO

Opinion surveys of Tokyo people show that:
- 90 percent worry that they won't be able to keep up their standard of living
- 74 percent worry about being replaced by computers and robots
- 80 percent worry that there may be a major earthquake soon

TOKYO PEOPLE

SHIGEO NAGASHIMA

A national sporting hero and much-loved figure, Nagashima was a star hitter with Tokyo's Giants baseball team and later their manager until he retired to become a TV commentator. He had been 12 years out of the game when the Giants ran into a bad patch and he was brought back at the age of 56 to restore their fortunes. It worked. In the first year they came in second in their league; the following season they won it and took the Japan Series finals as well.

KENZABURO OE

This prolific novelist was awarded the Nobel Prize for Literature in 1994, causing a run on his books in Japan where they had not been widely read before. Many of his compatriots find his interweaving of political themes and fantasy "difficult." He says he relates more to William Blake and James Joyce than to Japanese tradition. Oe has a severely handicapped son who as a baby seemed to respond only to sound, so he stimulated that capacity by playing him records of birdsong. The son is now a noted composer.

The novelist Kenzaburo Oe

YOTARO KOBAYASHI

The conservative economist and president of Fuji-Xerox, now in his fifties, is one of the leading figures in the Keidanren. This influential organization of business and industry chiefs had previously always been dominated by the bosses of the great *zaibatsu*, the heavy industry-banking conglomerates such as Mitsui, Mitsubishi, and Sumitomo.

MAKIKO TANAKA

The tough and boisterous daughter of former Liberal Democratic Party prime minister Kakuei Tanaka served as Minister of Science in the 1994 Murayama government. Steeped in politics from birth, she overcame her father's opposition and studied in the United States, becoming an accomplished speaker who says what she thinks—a quality almost unheard-of in Japanese women. Now a senator, she is spoken of as a possible future prime minister.

Woman in orbit

Science minister Makiko Tanaka's talk with Chiaki Mukai, the first Japanese woman astronaut, during the 15 days she spent orbiting in a US Space Shuttle in 1994, represented twin pinnacles of achievement for Japanese womanhood. A heart surgeon, Mukai is a heroine to many women who feel that they have not been able to realize their own potential. She is "more like a man," they say, revealingly.

A CHRONOLOGY

10,000–300BC	Jomon Period. Neolithic hunting and fishing culture; decorative pottery making
300BC–AD250	Yayoi Period. Immigrants from Asia introduce metal working and rice-paddy cultivation
250–710	Kofun Culture. From 300 to 400 gradual unification under Yamato clan, whose leader takes title of emperor. Yamato power declines 400–600. Growing influence of Chinese culture, and rapid spread of Buddhism
794	Imperial capital moves from Nara to Kyoto
850–1150	Advisors to the emperor acquire more and more power. Rise of the *samurai* (warrior) class
1192	Minamoto are victorious in a power struggle. Yoritomo Minamoto rules from Kamakura as *shogun* or warlord. The emperor in Kyoto becomes a virtual puppet
12th–16th centuries	Frequent civil wars between rival clans
1274 and 1281	Mongol invasion fleets destroyed by typhoons (*kamikaze* or "divine wind")
1336	Ashikaga Takauji takes over as *shogun* and establishes his rule in Kyoto
1543	A Portuguese ship makes the first landfall by Europeans on the coast of Japan
1572–1600	The warlord Nobunaga Oda seizes power in Kyoto. After his murder in 1582, Hideyoshi Toyotomi unites the whole country. On Hideyoshi's death (1598) a power struggle ensues between regional warlords
1600–1639	Ieyasu Tokugawa is victorious at the battle of Sekigahara (▶ 12). The Tokugawa shogunate is established (1603), with its capital at Edo (the future Tokyo). A long period of isolation from the outside world begins
1840s	Foreign countries press Japan to open its ports

1853 and 1858	A US fleet under Commodore Matthew Perry anchors in Tokyo Bay. Treaty of Kanagawa (now Yokohama) signed in 1858 opens ports to trade
1867–1868	Supporters of 15-year-old Emperor Meiji launch a *coup d'état* against the shogunate. Edo is renamed Tokyo ("Eastern Capital"). Shinto is declared the state religion
1894–1910	War with China (1894–1895) and Russia (1904–1905). In 1910 Japan annexes Korea
1926	Hirohito becomes emperor
1930s	Government is increasingly dominated by military leadership. Japan invades China (1937)
1940–1945	Economic sanctions imposed on Japan (1940). Next year Japan attacks Pearl Harbor and USA enters World War II. Defeat by the US navy in the battle of Midway marks the turning point of the war. In 1945 massive air raids destroy much of Tokyo. Atomic bombs are dropped on Hiroshima and Nagasaki. Japan surrenders
1945–1951	US General Douglas MacArthur rules as benevolent dictator. Emperor Hirohito renounces claim to divine status
1952	Restoration of Japanese independence
1960s	Rapid economic and industrial recovery. Tokyo hosts Olympic Games in 1964
1980s	Japan becomes the world's greatest trading nation. Tokyo's stock market booms. Emperor Akihito succeeds Hirohito in 1989
1991–1994	Recession. Stock market falls by 60 percent
1995	Earthquake destroys much of the port city of Kobe, inducing a shudder of fear in Tokyo
1995–1998	Unemployment grows as economy remains sluggish. Financial scandals and bankruptcies rock Tokyo

PEOPLE & EVENTS FROM HISTORY

IEYASU TOKUGAWA

As a child, the future ruler spent years as a hostage in the courts of rival clans. He grew up into a cunning, watchful, and ruthless leader.

Emperor Hirohito

After the death of Hideyoshi in 1598, as a member of the regency council Tokugawa was sworn to support the succession of Hideyoshi's young son, but mutual suspicion among the regents soon led to war. Ieyasu's forces were victorious at the battle of Sekigahara in 1600. He gradually suppressed all opposition and took the title of *shogun* in 1603. His stronghold of Edo (later renamed Tokyo) became the capital and the Tokugawa dynasty ruled Japan until 1867.

EMPEROR HIROHITO

A small, shy man whose appearance and manner belied his supposed divine status, Hirohito traveled widely in his youth and admired Western ways. But as emperor he remained passive as Japan's military leaders took the road to war. He spoke only vaguely to his ministers and never in public. Arguably his greatest service to his people was to order them to submit instead of fighting to the death. His 1945 radio broadcast calling on Japan to "endure the unendurable" and surrender was the first time that most of his subjects had ever heard his voice.

GENERAL DOUGLAS MACARTHUR

As Supreme Commander in Japan from 1945 to 1951, the charismatic, controversial American had absolute power, more than any ruler since the *shogun*s. Paradoxically, he used it to build a democracy. Taking over a starving wasteland, he rejected calls for the trial or removal of Hirohito and gained the confidence and cooperation of the Japanese people. His dismissal over the conduct of the Korean War caused widespread shock in Japan.

The pilot and the *shogun*

In April 1600, the lone surviving ship of a Dutch trading fleet reached Japan, sailed by a mere six men. One was an English pilot, Will Adams. He was taken to meet Ieyasu, who was eager to learn about European ways and who asked Adams to build him a ship. The pilot ("*Anjin-san*") spent the rest of his life serving the *shogun*s, dying in 1620. Readers of James Clavell's novel *Shogun* will recognize the story, although he changed names and invented many details.

TOKYO
how to organize your time

ITINERARIES

Some say the best thing to do in Tokyo is to take a trip out, but there's plenty to do in the city as well. After a quick look around the district where you are staying, make learning how to use the subway a top priority (► 90). Note that most museums and other attractions close on Mondays.

ITINERARY ONE	**PALACE GARDENS & GINZA**
Morning	Start where it all began, the site of the first Tokugawa *shogun*'s mighty Edo Castle, on a low hill in the Imperial Palace East Garden (► 36). Keen walkers could follow the moat to Hibiya Park (► 40) before penetrating the famous shopping and entertainment district of Ginza (► 41)
Lunch	Ginza's restaurants and department stores provide a wide choice of eating places
Afternoon	The fine Bridgestone Museum of Art (► 52), the Idemitsu Museum of Arts (► 52), and the Kabuki-za Theater (► 78) are a short walk away
Evening	You could spend a fortune on an evening in Ginza, but you don't have to: there are reasonably priced restaurants too
ITINERARY TWO	**TSUKIJI & ASAKUSA**
Morning	Get up very early (jetlag might make it easier) and go to the fish market at Tsukiji (► 44) Have a *sushi* breakfast in the market (or something more conventional) The Sumida river cruise leaves from the Hama Rikyu Garden (► 43) near Tsukiji, heading up river to Asakusa (► 49)
Lunch	There's a variety of places at Asakusa for a coffee, snack, or lunch
Afternoon	Energetic walkers can combine Asakusa and Ueno Park (► 17), with its museums and shrines
Evening	Spend the evening dining and checking out the nightlife in Roppongi (► 80)

ITINERARY THREE	**SHINJUKU & HARAJUKU**
Morning	You are bound to pass through the vast, frenetic Shinjuku Station (➤ 27) more than once. Stop off and take the west exit for the city's biggest camera stores (➤ 77) Continue on to the futuristic skyscrapers: the top of the new City Hall (➤ 26) gives the best views
Lunch	Return to the station for snack and lunch options galore
Afternoon	Harajuku (➤ 31) is a starting point for visiting the Meiji Shrine (➤ 30), Ota Museum (➤ 52–53), and Sunday teenage capers in Yoyogi Park (➤ 59)
Evening	East of Shinjuku Station the narrow streets of Kabukicho (➤ 80) are a focus of nightlife and low life
ITINERARY FOUR	**LOOSE ENDS**
Morning	Now that you're an expert, use the subway system to get around to places you have missed Visit the controversial Yasukuni Shrine (➤ 38) Look at the view from Tokyo Tower (➤ 34), and take in nearby Zojoji Temple (➤ 35) Marvel at *samurai* values at Sengakuji Temple (➤ 33)
Lunch	Drop into any convenient noodle bar
Afternoon	Tokyo Disneyland (➤ 50) is good entertainment—not only for children— and only 15 minutes by train from Tokyo Station
Evening	The evening scene in Shibuya is as much fun as anywhere in Tokyo, less artificial than Ginza, more Japanese than Roppongi The new development at Yebisu (➤ 32), one stop away on the JR line, is well worth a visit for its restaurants, beer hall, and museums

15

WALKS

Sumida River and the Asahi Brewery (right)

A WALK AROUND ASAKUSA & KAPPABASHI

At the pier or the exit from Asakusa subway station, look across the Sumida River to see the controversial Asahi Brewery buildings designed by Philippe Starck.

Two blocks from the river, Kaminarimon is one of the gates to Sensoji (or Asakusa Kannon) Temple. Through it, the pedestrian Nakamise-dori is lined with small shops. Take note of the street to the left, Denboin-dori, before touring the temple precinct. Return to Denboin-dori, which leads to the entertainment district, with theaters and plenty of places to eat. The Nakase restaurant (► 65), on the first corner, is noted for *tempura*. More economical are the noodle shops on the side streets. Hanayashiki, behind the temple, is a children's amusement park.

Cut through to the west, away from the temple, to the Asakusa View tower on the broad Kokusai-dori. Turn left along Kokusai-dori for one block and then right for 300 yards, past two temples, to meet the main street of Kappabashi, famous for its shops selling kitchen equipment and supplies, including the plastic replica food seen in window displays. Turn left (south) and continue to Asakusa-dori: the intersection is marked by a giant chef's head. A right turn brings you to Inaricho subway station.

A WALK AROUND UENO & YANAKA

Ueno is one of the city's busiest hubs. The east exit from the JR station leads to Showa-dori, in the shadow of an elevated expressway. Turn left (north) and you will quickly be in so-called "motorcycle heaven" (➤ 72). Retrace your steps to the main road junction south of the station and look for the archway leading to Ameyoko, Tokyo's liveliest market, with thousands of stalls stretching as far as Okachimachi JR Station. At the Ueno end of the market, cross Chuo-dori and enter Ueno Park at its southeast corner where the Shitamachi folk museum faces Shinobazu Pond, home to hosts of waterbirds.

Yanaka bric-a-brac shop

There is plenty more to see in the park. You can visit as many of its shrines and museums as you have time for. At its northern end, turn left as you face the Tokyo National Museum. Passing the Fine Arts University, you leave the park and enter Yanaka, whose narrow streets, old shops, and houses escaped the 1923 earthquake and 1945 bombing. With dozens of temples and attractive gardens, this is more

like old Kyoto than Tokyo. You will probably get lost here, but it hardly matters—the cemetery is one landmark; to the north, Nippori JR Station is another. Aim to finish at Nezu subway station on the western edge of Yanaka.

A traditional house in Yanaka

THE SIGHTS

- Ameyoko market (➤ 72)
- Ueno Park (➤ 59)
- Shitamachi Museum (➤ 48)
- Tokyo National Museum (➤ 46)
- Yanaka streets and houses
- Yanaka cemetery

INFORMATION

Distance 5 miles
Time 2 ½ hours
Start point Ueno JR Station
➕ L2
🚃 Ueno (Yamanote Line)
🚇 Ueno (Ginza Line)
End point Nezu subway station
➕ K1
🚇 Nezu
Note: Museums in Ueno Park close Mon (or Tue if Mon is a national holiday)

17

EVENING STROLLS

INFORMATION

Ginza
Distance 1.2 miles
Time 1½ hours
Start point Higashi-Ginza subway station
➕ K7
🚇 Higashi-Ginza
End point Yurakucho station
➕ K6
🚇 Yurakucho
🚃 Yurakucho

In the early evening, many shops are still open and people pack into bars and restaurants; around 11PM they all pour out again.

Shinjuku-Kabukicho
Distance 1.2 miles
Time 1½ hours
Start and end point Shinjuku Station (east exit)
➕ D4
🚇 Shinjuku
🚃 Shinjuku

Early in the evening, people stroll about, deciding where to go. Later, the usually amiable drunks reel their way home, or to a hotel.

A traditional orchestra plays for kabuki *theater*

AROUND GINZA

At Higashi-Ginza station, take a look at the Kabuki-za Theater (➤ 78) before heading up Harumi-dori toward the bright lights of the main Ginza crossing with Chuo-dori. Some of the biggest stores are on this avenue, but it's worth diverting into as many of the narrow side streets as time and energy allow. The rectangular street pattern makes it difficult to get lost. The price of real estate around here means that no site is wasted. Back on Harumi-dori, you could finish your walk and take the subway at Ginza, or continue to Yurakucho where there are reasonably priced places to eat near the station and under the tracks.

AROUND SHINJUKU-KABUKICHO

Tokyo's most varied "entertainment district" starts just east of the station (subway or JR). Some signs mention Kabukicho but if you don't see one, turn left towards the Shinjuku Prince tower. Spread out to the right of it is a maze of narrow streets lined by bars, strip joints, massage parlors, even some good restaurants. If you go through the doors of any establishment, ask the price first—of everything—or you could be in for a shock, but unlike the low-life areas of most cities, there's practically no street crime. The big Koma theater is a landmark. North and east of it things get raunchier, and then peter out into anonymity. Turn back and, if in doubt, ask for *Shinjuku Eki* (station).

ORGANIZED SIGHTSEEING

Sightseeing tours are somewhat expensive—roughly ¥4,500 for a half-day, ¥11,000 for a full day with lunch, ¥12,000 for a night tour with dinner—but they'll save your shoe leather. Tour companies pick you up at the main hotels but may not bring you back there: some tours end in Ginza. You can check on the choice and the prices at the TIC (➤ 91) or at hotel desks. The main tour companies are Japan Gray Line Co. Ltd. ✉ 3-3-3 Nishi-Shinbashi, Minato-ku ☎ 3433–5475, and Sunrise Tours, Japan Travel Bureau Inc. ✉ 5-5-2 Kiba, Koto-ku ☎ 5620–9500.

The Ginza district

CITY TOURS

The traffic makes the time you have at the various stops unpredictable, but sights frequently included are the Imperial Palace East Garden, Meiji Shrine, Tokyo Tower, and Asakusa, the last sometimes reached by the Sumida river bus. Morning or afternoon tours are offered, or all-day packages including lunch. Some tours offer a taste of culture, with demonstrations of Japanese flower-arranging, doll-making, or a tea ceremony.

An Industrial Tokyo tour may take you to Japan Airlines maintenance base at Haneda Airport, the Kirin Brewery, or the Isuzu car factory. A tour to Tokyo Disneyland (➤ 50) gives you seven hours in the park, and unlimited rides, but you can easily do this on your own.

OUT-OF-TOWN TOURS

Excursions are available to Kamakura (➤ 20), Hakone (➤ 21), and Nikko. One-day combinations of Kamakura and Hakone are too rushed to be recommended. There are tours to Kyoto (➤ 22–23) for one or two days, or as part of a combination vacation of any desired length.

Tokyo by night

The evening tours you will see widely advertised generally combine dinner with a show. You have a choice of menus, perhaps *sukiyaki, kushiage* (➤ 64), or steak, and of entertainment. Some tours offer a chance to sample *kabuki* theater (➤ 78) and traditional *geisha* entertainment of music, song, and conversation. Others may take you to a Western-style revue with cabaret acts and perhaps topless dancers, but nothing more risqué.

19

EXCURSIONS

INFORMATION

Kamakura
Distance 30 miles
Time About 1 hour from Tokyo

⊙ Sites vary. Typically:
Mar–Sep daily 8–5.
Oct–Feb daily 8–4

🍴 Around Kamakura Station and along Wakamiya Avenue

🚉 Kita-kamakura, Kamakura, or Hase from Tokyo Station, lower level Track 1 (JR Yokosuka Line), or at intermediate stops, Shinbashi or Shinagawa

♿ Few (difficult access, hilly sites)

💴 Fare moderate; entrance fees expensive

❓ Day tours from Tokyo only visit major sites. Area is well signposted in English. The Kamakura Information Center at Kamakura Station sells maps of the area

KAMAKURA

Tokyo seems far away as the train passes through the wooded slopes that surround Kamakura on three sides, with the sea on the fourth. The military ruler Minamoto Yoritomo set up his base here in 1192, leaving the emperor as a figurehead in Kyoto, and Kamakura remained the seat of power until 1333. Its many shrines and temples are quite spread out, but the railroad can cut down the amount of walking.

Near Hase Station The Great Buddha (*Daibutsu*) at Kotokuin Temple is second in size to Nara's, but is a finer sculpture. Cast in bronze in 1252, the 37-foot statue is hollow; you can climb inside. Hasedera Temple on a nearby hillside houses a 30-foot-high wooden carving of Kannon, said to have been washed ashore over 1,000 years ago. Infinitely touching are the countless tiny images of Jizo at the Zojoji Temple (► 35).

Near Kamakura Station The wide Wakamiya ("Young Prince") Avenue leads from the sea to Hachimangu Shrine, by way of the steep Drum Bridge. Near the shrine, Kamakura Museum houses relics of the era of its glory and some fine woodblock prints.

Near Kita-kamakura Station The 13th-century Engakuji Temple is one of the most important Zen Buddhist temples in Japan. Close by, the neighboring Tokeiji Temple was once the only refuge available to women fleeing cruel husbands.

The Hachimangu Shrine

The mountainous area west of Tokyo, with lakes and countless hot springs, is a favorite weekend target of local day-trippers. Try to go midweek and avoid peak holiday times (► 24).

HAKONE

Unless you travel by car (recommended only out of season), use the network of public transportation (see panel). From Hakone-Yumoto, the Hakone Tozan Railroad zigzags over the mountains, making stops on the way. Miyanoshita is a resort with thermal pools. Next to Chokoku-no-Mori Station is Hakone Open Air Museum, with a spectacular sculpture garden and gallery. From the last station, Gora, a cable car soars over Owakudani valley, where sulfurous fumes and smoke pour from a dozen crevices. Stop here and eat eggs boiled in the hot springs. Another 25 minutes by cable car takes you to Togendai, the base for cruises on Lake Ashi.

MOUNT FUJI (FUJI-YAMA)

For most visitors, a view of the perfect volcanic cone is enough, especially as reflected in Lake Ashi. If you want to see it close up, head for Kawaguchiko. Gogome, closer still, is the main starting point for climbers. The season is short (July 1 to August 31) and weather can be bad, so be prepared. The climb to the summit (12,388 feet) takes 4–5 hours, the descent rather less.

INFORMATION

Hakone
Distance 56 miles
Time 1½ hours from Tokyo, then 55 minutes on local train
🕐 Open Air Museum: Mar–Oct 9–5. Nov–Feb 9–4
🍴 At and near stations
🚆 Hakone-Yumote (Limited Express from Shinjuku Station, Odakyu Line)
🚾 Good
💰 Fares and entrance fees expensive
❓ On Hakone Tozan Railroad, a "Hakone Free Pass" (not free) covers four days' travel by trains, buses, cable car, boats

Mount Fuji
Distance 60 miles
Time 2 hours from Tokyo
🍴 At stations; none on mountain
🚆 Kawaguchiko (Odakyu Line from Shinjuku Station; change at Otsuki)
🚾 Few
💰 Fares expensive
❓ Tours; buses also run from Shinjuku to Kawaguchiko

Mount Fuji and Lake Ashi

EXCURSIONS

Downtown Kyoto

KYOTO

Kyoto, 318 miles from Tokyo, was Japan's capital for more than 1,000 years, the home of the emperor even while power resided elsewhere. It became the chief center of art and religion, and remained the cultural focus even after it ceased to be the capital in 1868. It was spared the bombing that devastated most Japanese cities in 1945.

Don't be put off by first impressions. The area around the station looks like any modern Japanese city, but a short walk away are narrow old streets and traditional shops. Kyoto National Museum has fine archaeological and art collections. The Imperial Palace in the center of the city, built in 1855, soon lost its role when the emperor moved to Tokyo. Of more interest is Nijo Castle, built in 1603 by the *shogun* Ieyasu Tokugawa (➤ 12), to mark his seizure of power. Most temples and shrines are on the outskirts of the city, but easily accessible. Only a few can be mentioned here.

Kiyomizu-dera Beautifully positioned on a hillside, this temple ("Clear Water") has a famous wide veranda giving a view over the city. Its pagoda, painted bright vermilion on the underside, is a landmark.

Chion-in The chief temple of the Buddhist Jodo sect is enormous, and brilliantly painted and decorated. The main buildings date from the 17th century. The belfry houses the biggest bell in Japan, cast in 1633 and needing the efforts of 17 men to ring it.

Heian Shrine The massive *torii* (gate) and shrine buildings are quite modern, built in 1895 to mark the 1,100th anniversary of the

INFORMATION

Distance 318 miles

Time 2 hours 37 minutes by bullet train (*shinkansen*)

✉ Tourist Information Center (TIC): Kyoto Tower, Higashi-Shiokojicho, Shimogyo-ku, Kyoto

☎ TIC: 075/371–5649

🕐 Sites: vary. Typically: Mar–Oct 9–5. Nov–Feb 9–4. TIC: Mon–Fri 9–5; Sat 9–12

🍴 Plenty at and near station, in city and near major shrines

🚉 Kyoto (from Tokyo Station)

♿ Few

💰 Fares expensive; entrance fees moderate to expensive

❓ Tours from Tokyo (day tour too rushed) and within Kyoto. Avoid weekends and peak holiday periods. Arrange accommodations in advance, or at TIC early in the day. Good free maps; city guide in English

founding of Kyoto, but they are intended to echo the style of the first imperial palace. The gardens are famous for their spring blossom and for the color of their autumn leaves.

The huge torii at the entrance to Heian Shrine

Ginkakuji (Silver Pavilion) This was built as a villa for a retired 15th-century *shogun*, Yoshimasa Ashikaga, whose intention to cover it with silver was never carried out, although the name stuck. In the other original building, the Togudo, Yoshimasa devised the tea ceremony that is performed to this day. The gardens are renowned for their ascetic formality and balance.

Kinkakuji (Golden Pavilion) Built in 1397 as a country retreat for a *shogun*, this three-story jewel covered in gold leaf became a temple after his death. What you see now is a replica: the original was destroyed in a fire started by a disturbed priest in 1950.

Ryoanji Temple Zen Garden *Aficionados* will argue endlessly over the merits of raked gravel and carefully positioned rocks, the features of this austere garden. Most foreigners are politely mystified.

Kyoto transportation

The city is bigger than it looks.

- **Walking** from one shrine or garden to others nearby is delightful, but a route linking the important sights would be 12 miles long.
- A **bicycle** is a good way to get around: ask at the TIC.
- Public **buses** cover all areas. The TIC has a route map.
- The **subway** runs north–south through the center and is not very useful.
- Two private **railways** connect a number of sights.
- **Tour buses** are expensive and visit only a few sights.

23

What's On

Some dates mentioned below may vary from year to year.

JANUARY
Parade of Firemen (Jan 6): Acrobatic displays on the top of tall bamboo ladders on Chuo-dori, Harumi

Young Adults' Day (Jan 15): Tens of thousands of 20-year-olds troop to the Meiji Shrine (➤ 30), the young women dressed in their finest kimonos

FEBRUARY
Setsubun Bean-Throwing festival (Feb 3 or 4): Held at many shrines and temples to welcome spring and invite good fortune

MARCH
Doll festival (Mar 3): Displays of dolls

APRIL
Golden Days holiday (end Apr to first week in May): Millions of people travel to their family homes or on vacation

MAY
Sanja Matsuri (third weekend May): Three-day festival and parades of portable shrines at Asakusa Kannon (Sensoji) Temple (➤ 49)

JUNE
Sanno Matsuri festival (Jun 10–16): At Hie Jinja, parades and processions carry portable shrines through Akasaka

JULY
Great Market at Asakusa Kannon Temple (Jul 10): Portable shrine is carried in procession

O-Bon (week of Jul 15): Buddhist temple festivals honor the dead. *O-Bon* dance parties are staged in many communities

Floating Lanterns (Jul 17): On Shinobazu Pond, Ueno Park

AUGUST
Fukugawa River festival (Aug 14–15): Ⓜ Monzen Nakacho Station, Tozai Line

OCTOBER
Oeshiki Festival (Oct 11–13): Procession of lanterns at Hommonji Buddhist Temple

NOVEMBER
Emperor Meiji's birthday festival (Nov 3): At Meiji Shrine

Shichi-go-san (Nov 3): Children aged 7, 5, and 3—many of them dressed in traditional kimonos—are taken to shrines

DECEMBER
Gishi-sai (evening of Dec 14): Honors the 47 *ronin* at Sengakuji Temple (➤ 33)

Battledore Fair (Dec 17–19): At Asakusa Kannon Temple

Emperor's Birthday (Dec 23): Opening of Imperial Palace grounds

New Year holiday (Dec 28–Jan 3): Business shuts down and many leisure facilities are closed

TOKYO's
top 25 sights

*The sights are shown on the inside front cover and inside back cover,
numbered* **1–25** *from west to east across the city*

1

METROPOLITAN GOVERNMENT OFFICES

HIGHLIGHTS

- The 45th-floor observatories, 663 feet high
- Surreal skyscrapers of Shinjuku
- Views of parks and distant downtown area
- Glimpse of Mount Fuji (one day in five)
- Sunset and night views
- Multiscreen video history
- Sculptures of human figures in plaza
- Exterior granite, white from Spain, dark from Sweden

INFORMATION

- ✚ C4
- ✉ Tokyo Metropolitan Government Offices, 2-8-1 Nishi-Shinjuku, Shinjuku-ku
- ☎ 5321–1111
- 🕐 Tue–Fri 9:30–5:30; Sat, Sun, and national holidays 9:30–7:30. Closed Mon (or Tue if Mon a national holiday), and Dec 29–Jan 3
- 🍴 Snack bar on 45th floor; countless restaurants in nearby buildings
- 🚇 Shinjuku
- 🚉 Shinjuku
- ♿ Very good
- 🎟 Free
- ↔ Shinjuku Station (➤ 27), Japanese Sword Museum (➤ 29)

Above: the twin towers of the Metropolitan Government Offices

This glittering monster was planned in the boom years of the 1980s, when anything seemed possible, and opened in 1991. The view from the top is unrivaled and pure 21st century, with silver and black towers rising from windswept plazas.

Vantage point Each of the twin towers of Building No. 1 has an observatory on the 45th floor. It makes no difference which tower you choose: the elevators whisk you to the top in less than a minute. On a clear day the view is the most spectacular in Tokyo, with futuristic skyscrapers in the foreground, the green islands of the Meiji Shrine Inner Garden and Shinjuku Garden beyond, and the Imperial Palace, Ginza, and Tokyo Bay to the east. If you are lucky you'll see Mount Fuji's perfect cone far away on the southwestern horizon.

Growth area In the days of the shogunate, Shinjuku was still a day's march from the capital, Edo (now Tokyo). Weary travelers coming from the west would stop at its inns to bathe and rest, dine, and visit one of the many houses of pleasure. With the coming of the railways, Shinjuku became a major junction. As late as 1970, Shinjuku was known mainly for its station, red-light district, and sewage farm— since banished. When investors looked for alternatives to central Tokyo, Shinjuku had an important advantage: it seemed to survive earthquakes better than other areas. The first highrise was the Keio Plaza Hotel, put up by one of the railroad-department store combines. The Mitsui and Sumitomo office buildings soon followed. Then the city government decided to move to Shinjuku and commissioned Kenzo Tange to design this grandiose complex, on a scale to match its 7-trillion-yen annual budget.

2

SHINJUKU STATION (SHINJUKU EKI)

Twice a day, a tidal wave of humanity pours through Japan's busiest station. Two to three million commuters, shoppers, and schoolchildren stream along its underground passages, heading for a dozen exits, or just changing trains.

Human anthill Subway lines and JR railway lines meet at Shinjuku, plus the private lines feeding customers to their own department stores right above the station. The famous people-pushers operate at rush hour (*rashawa* in Japanese), packing as many bodies as they can into each carriage, giving them a final shove to let the doors close and then bowing as the train pulls out. It's worth experiencing—once—but not as an introduction to the system. Learn your way around at a quieter time first.

Exits You can walk more than a half a mile underground (much more if you get lost). One long concourse on the west side links the station complex to many of Shinjuku's skyscrapers. Here and there, the homeless, who have somehow dropped through the cracks of Japan's tightly knit society, find a place to sleep, cocooned in cardboard cartons. To the hurrying crowds they seem invisible. The east exit leads to several stories of good eating places in the My City building, and into a maze of alleys and the varied night entertainment of Kabukicho.

HIGHLIGHTS

- Organized chaos of rush hour
- People-pushers
- Over 2 million commuters a day
- My City restaurant complex
- Department stores above station
- Underground city
- Harangues by fringe groups of far right and left
- Camera stores near station
- Kabukicho nightlife
- Times Square development on south side of station

INFORMATION

- ✚ D4
- ✉ Shinjuku-ku
- ⏱ 4:30AM–1AM
- 🍴 Innumerable eating places of every kind
- 🚇 Shinjuku
- 🚆 Shinjuku
- ♿ Few
- 🎟 Free
- ↔ Metropolitan Government Offices (➤ 26), Kabukicho (➤ 80)

3

SHINJUKU NATIONAL GARDEN

HIGHLIGHTS

- 150 acres, beautifully landscaped
- Ponds, bridges, and shaded glades
- Japanese garden
- French garden
- English garden
- Greenhouse of tropical plants and flowers
- Fall chrysanthemum shows
- Autumn colors
- Picnic parties under the spring blossoms

INFORMATION

- ✚ E5
- ✉ 11 Naitocho, Shinjuku-ku
- ☎ 3350–0151
- ◷ 9–4:30. Closed Mon except at cherry-blossom time
- 🍴 Snacks
- Ⓖ Shinjuku Gyoen-mae. Take the south exit and turn right
- 🚃 Shinjuku
- ♿ Few
- 💵 Moderate

Shinjuku National Garden (Shinjuku Gyoen) is the perfect place for a stroll at most times of the year, but it is especially worth a visit in the spring when thousands come to walk and picnic under their beloved flowering cherry trees.

Origins The Shinjuku garden is one of the surpisingly large green spaces that relieve the concrete monotony of the city. It was once the estate of the powerful leader (*daimyo*) of the Naito clan—one of the Tokugawa shoguns who parceled out the land around their Edo stronghold to lesser lords whose duty was to defend the approaches. Following the overthrow of the shogunate and restoration of imperial power in 1868, it came into the hands of the emperor. After World War II, it was opened to the public as a national park.

Garden sights Landscaped with little hills, ponds, and bridges, the park includes greenhouses filled with tropical plants, an English country garden, a French formal garden, and a Japanese garden with a Chinese-style pavilion.

At cherry-blossom time large crowds—guided by daily blossom reports on TV—are drawn to see almost 2,000 trees, their white or pink petals blowing like snow in the wind. The biggest, most perfect blooms of Japan's national flower, the chrysanthemum, are on show September to November.

The English garden in Shinjuku National Garden

JAPANESE SWORD MUSEUM

Gleaming and flawless, the mirror-smooth blades kept here are up to 900 years old, deadly weapons transmuted by their age and beauty into works of art. It is easy to understand why they were credited with magical power.

The museum A box-shaped building on stilts, hidden in a residential street southwest of the Shinjuku skyscrapers, holds some of Japan's most revered cultural treasures. If you enjoy walking, visit the Sword Museum on the way between Shinjuku and the northwestern gate of the Meiji Shrine garden. You will need to ask the way. If you don't speak any Japanese, just say *Bijutsu Token*, or draw a picture of a curved blade and show it to a policeman or anybody who looks helpful.

The art The atmosphere inside is almost religious, the handful of visitors gazing in awe at swords that probably sliced off *samurai* heads. The armor on display shows the defensive measures taken to try to ward off the flashing blades, including plenty of padding around the neck. Amazingly detailed leaflets in English explain the complex terminology and manu-facture. Repeated folding and hammering produces a layered, resilient steel blade. This is coated in clay, except for the edge, heated in the furnace, and plunged into cold water. Thus tempered, the edge becomes diamond hard, able to cut through bone and inferior metal. Some sword-masters from as early as the 12th and 13th centuries signed their work, but others can be identified from the wavy tempering patterns along the blades. Several of the blades on display have been declared "National Treasures," quite literally beyond price as nothing like them would ever come onto the market.

HIGHLIGHTS

- 12th-century Heian period *tachi* sword
- 13th- to 14th-century Kamakura-period swords
- 17th-century Edo-period decorative swords
- Full *samurai* armor
- Decorated stirrups
- Display on swordmaking
- Explanation of hardening and tempering
- Scabbard collection

INFORMATION

- ✚ C5
- ✉ 4-25-10 Yoyogi, Shibuya-ku
- ☎ 3379–1386
- ◷ 9–4. Closed Mon, and Dec 28–Jan 4
- 🚃 Sangubashi (Odakyu Line)
- ♿ Good
- ✋ Moderate
- ↔ Metropolitan Government Offices (➤ 26), Meiji Shrine (➤ 30)

A protective samurai *helmet*

5

MEIJI SHRINE (MEIJI JINGU)

- 175 acres of wooded park
- Giant *torii* (gates)
- Shrine hall of cypress wood
- Folded paper prayers on bushes
- Cherry blossoms in spring
- Iris garden in summer
- Winter ice carvings
- Treasure Museum
- Wedding processions

INFORMATION

- ✚ D6
- ✉ 1-1 Yoyogi, Shibuya-ku
- 🕑 Sunrise–sunset. Closed third Fri of each month
- 🚇 Meijijingu-mae
- 🚆 Harajuku (JR), Sangubashi (Odakyu Line)
- ♿ Few
- ✋ Free
- ↔ Japanese Sword Museum (➤ 29), Harajuku (➤ 31), Yoyogi Park (➤ 31), Ota Museum (➤ 52–53)

The Meiji Shrine

It's a pleasure to walk through the woods to this national focus of the Shinto religion. Here, people mark important stages of their lives. Babies are brought for their first temple visit and newlyweds come to have their marriages blessed.

The shrine The reign of Emperor Meiji (1868–1912) saw Japan transformed from a medieval to a modern state. The shrine was built in 1920 to honor him and his empress: in accordance with the beliefs of the day they had been declared divine. It was destroyed by fire in the air raids of 1945, but rebuilt in the original classical design. The great *torii* (gates) are made from 1,700-year-old cypress trees from Taiwan. More than 100,000 seedlings sent from all over Japan have since grown into a forest. The Treasure Museum at the northern end of the gardens houses some of the royal clothes and personal possessions.

Occasions Babies dressed in their best are usually brought by proud parents on Thursdays, and you can often see wedding processions, some in traditional costume and some in Western dress. The main festival is on November 3, Emperor Meiji's birthday.

HARAJUKU

The street scene is a bizarre parade of the young and would-be young, in black leather and tiny miniskirts even on arctic days. Hair is greased back into a 1950s style, bleached blond or dyed green—and that's on the boys.

East of the station Across the street from Harajuku Station, Takeshita-dori is a magnet for teenagers, an alley lined by stalls selling colored glasses, music tapes, fast food, coffee, and clothing at prices that are bargains, at least by Tokyo standards. For something more elegant, and expensive, look in the boutiques on the parallel street, the tree-lined Omotesando-dori. The Ota Museum (➤ 52–53), just off it, houses a superb collection of *ukiyo-e* (woodblock prints; ➤ 53, panel). One of the city's best antiques and flea markets is held on the first and fourth Sundays of each month, near the Togo Shrine (➤ 57) just off Meiji-dori. The shrine itself honors the admiral who was the architect of the Japanese navy that defeated the Russian fleet in 1905.

Yoyogi Park The green space west of the station was once a Japanese army camp, and then the base of US occupying forces after World War II. Then it was the site of the 1964 Olympic Games village and retains the sports arenas built at the same time. Every Sunday, along the road from Harajuku crossing, a cacophony of competing rock bands rends the air, mime artists and acrobats entertain the crowds, and self-absorbed dancers go through their routines. They've been doing it for years: the rebellious look is largely fake and most will be back at their office jobs on Monday. Food stalls do a brisk trade in noodles and tasty stuffed pancakes. By 5 o'clock it's all over and the pent-up traffic is released onto the road.

HIGHLIGHTS

- Takeshita-dori street market
- Omotesando-dori high-fashion shops
- Ota Museum's woodblock prints
- Togo Shrine
- Sunday flea markets
- Yoyogi Park, gardens
- Sports center
- NHK Broadcasting Center tours (➤ 62)
- Sunday performers
- Teen fashion scene

INFORMATION

- ✛ D6/E7
- ✉ Harajuku, Shibuya-ku
- ⏰ 24 hours
- 🍴 A very wide choice
- 🚇 Meijijingu-mae
- 🚆 Harajuku
- ♿ Few
- ✋ Free
- ↔ Meiji Shrine (➤ 30), Ota Museum (➤ 52–53)

Above: the Togo Shrine, off Meiji-dori

7

YEBISU GARDEN PLACE

The old Sapporo Brewery site is one of Tokyo's most imaginative developments. A few years ago there was no reason to come here; now there are two brilliantly designed museums, a vast Bavarian beer hall, and a luxury hotel.

HIGHLIGHTS

- Museum of Photography visual tricks
- History of Images display
- Early photographic equipment
- Gallery of 1920s and 1930s photographs
- Beer museum
- HDTV and "virtual reality" demonstrations
- "Top of Yebisu" views
- Westin Tokyo Hotel
- Ersatz 1930s German beer hall

INFORMATION

- ✚ E10/F9
- ✉ 1 Mita, Meguro-ku and 4 Ebisu, Shibuya-ku
- ☎ Many different numbers for different functions
- ◉ Tue–Wed, Sat–Sun 10–6; Thu–Fri 10–8. Museums: closed Mon
- ∏ Beer hall; restaurants; fast-food outlets
- 🚇 Ebisu
- 🚉 Ebisu
- ♿ Good
- ⛲ Free (except Museum of Photography)
- ❓ Chain of moving walkways from JR Ebisu Station. Maps and signs say Ebisu for the area and station, Yebisu for the development

The beer connection As a serious polluter, the red-brick brewery had to go, but the company held on to the site, moved its offices here, and built 1,000 luxury apartments. Instead of being scrapped, some of the brewing equipment formed the basis of a beer museum, where it takes on the quality of sculpture. The brewing process is explained and in a "virtual reality" experience you can feel like a molecule going through fermentation yourself, before you sample a glass of the product (► 61).

Museum of Photography Tokyo Metropolitan Museum of Photography (► 54) showcases the latest photographic techniques and there are displays of historic equipment. The English explanations are excellent. The permanent collection of early photographs is an eye-opener.

Time out Along with the Mitsukoshi department store, there's a big restaurant complex with a huge beer hall reminiscent of a Munich *bierkeller* of the 1930s. Also visit the Westin Tokyo Hotel to see its opulent décor or take in the view from the bar or restaurant on the 22nd floor.

A mash copper in the Beer Museum

8

SENGAKUJI TEMPLE

This place offers an insight into Japanese values: the heroes commemorated are still honored for their loyalty, single-mindedness, efficiency, ruthlessness—and collective action. They lived and died by the rigid samurai code.

Code of honor Sengakuji was one of the three great temples of Edo, and it is still one of the most important in Tokyo. After their lord Naganori Asano was unjustly forced into suicide in 1701, Yoshitaka Oishi and 47 loyal retainers (*ronin*, meaning "masterless *samurai*") vowed to avenge him. They raided the castle of the chief instigator, Yoshinaka Kira, beheaded him, and carried the head in triumph to Asano's tomb at Sengakuji. They in turn were required by their code to commit ritual suicide, a duty they accepted as an honor. Before killing himself, Oishi chivalrously returned Kira's head to his family. The receipt for "one head" signed by the temple priests who took charge of it can still be seen in the museum. The story spread quickly and has captured Japanese imaginations ever since. It has been told and retold as *kabuki* (➤ 78) and puppet theater, in movies, and on television.

The tombs and museum Oishi and his followers were all buried at Sengakuji. The 47 simple stones are arranged in a square, with the larger tombs of Asano and his wife, and Oishi and his son, nearby. Clouds of smoke rise from incense sticks placed in front of each tomb by the many worshippers who come to honor the dead heroes. In the museum, polychrome statues believed to be exact likenesses of the 47 are so detailed that you can study every aspect of their dress. Their own armor and weapons, including some fiercesome spiked maces, are displayed separately.

HIGHLIGHTS

- Sanmon, the main gate
- Shoro, the Bell Tower
- Tombs of the 47 *ronin*
- Tombs of Asano and Oishi
- Temple gardens
- Polychrome statues of the 47 *ronin*
- *Samurai* weapons and armor
- Original clothing

INFORMATION

- ➕ H10
- ✉ 2-11-1 Takanawa, Minato-ku
- ☎ 3441–2208
- 🕐 9–4
- 🍴 Small restaurants in nearby street
- 🚇 Sengakuji (exit A2 and head uphill)
- ♿ Few
- 🎫 Temple: free. Museum: inexpensive

Above: tombstones at Sengakuji Temple

9

TOKYO TOWER

HIGHLIGHTS

- Observation decks at 492 feet and 820 feet
- General view from 820 feet
- View of Mount Fuji (one day in four)
- Holographic zone (3F)
- Aquarium (1F)
- Towerland electric arcade

INFORMATION

- ➕ H8
- ✉ 4-2-8 Shiba Koen (Park), Minato-ku
- ☎ 3433–5111
- 🕐 Mar 16–Nov 15 daily 9–8 (Aug 9–9). Nov 16–Mar 15 daily 9–7
- 🍴 Snack bars and cafés
- Ⓜ Kamiyacho, Onarimon
- ♿ Few (possible to first level)
- ✋ Expensive
- ↔ Zojoji Temple (➤ 35)

Tokyo's version of the Eiffel Tower out-does the original in height by a margin of about 30 feet. Choose a clear day for a fine view of the Sumida River and Tokyo Bay, Ginza, and the Imperial Palace.

The tower At Kamiyacho subway station, emerge from Exit 1 and head uphill. It takes about seven minutes to walk to the foot of the tower. Built in 1958 to carry television transmissions, it now broadcasts all eight of Tokyo's channels as well as FM radio stations. Cameras at the 820-foot level keep an eye on the city's notorious traffic and send pictures to a central control room, which is the source of the information flashed up along the expressways. The tower is the world's tallest free-standing iron structure. The view from the 492-foot level is not remarkable; you need to pay the

The view from the 1,092-foot-high Tokyo Tower

extra charge to go to 820 feet if the day is clear enough to make it worth while.

The extras Around the base and at the lower levels is a mixed bag of attractions, for which you have to pay substantial extra charges. An aquarium holds 50,000 fish of some 800 varieties, with many colorful species on sale at the aquarium shop. You can walk right through apparently solid objects in the holography display. TEPCO, the electric company, runs a play area with video games and a 3D movie theater.

ZOJOJI TEMPLE

Here, rows of little statues of Jizobosatsu (the protector of the souls of stillborn children), some dressed in baby clothes, hold whirling toy windmills. The sight is one of the city's oddest and most touching.

The temple Zojoji, the chief temple of the Jodo-Buddhist sect, was founded in 1393. It was the family temple of the Tokugawa clan, and when Ieyasu Tokugawa became *shogun* with Edo (Tokyo) as his power base, he set about enlarging and beautifying it. The Sanmon, the main gate built in 1605 in Chinese Tang Dynasty style, is a rare example of early Edo-period architecture left in Tokyo. All the other buildings at Zojoji were destroyed in the 1945 air raids and were later replaced by concrete replicas. An ancient black image of Amita Buddha is carried in procession three times a year, on January 15, May 15, and September 15.

The gardens Near the Sanmon, a cedar tree planted by President Ulysses S. Grant in 1879 also miraculously survived the 1945 air raids and fires. As at many temples, prayers on folded paper are tied like white flowers to the smaller trees and bushes. Nearby, the outlines of two feet said to be those of Buddha are incised in a rock that was probably brought from China (like similar work in the Tokyo National Museum). Also in the garden is a large temple bell, said to have been cast in 1673 from the ornamental hairpins of court ladies. Colorful and sad at the same time are the multiple images of Jizobosatsu, or Jizo, the Buddhist equivalent of an angel, dressed in red baby bonnets. Mothers who have experienced stillbirth, or an abortion, may dedicate an image of the deity and decorate it with baby clothes, toys, and little windmills.

HIGHLIGHTS

- Sanmon, the restored 1605 gate
- Main hall of the temple
- Great Bell of 1673, 10 feet high
- Cedar tree planted by President Grant
- Stone engraving of Buddha's feet
- Gardens, flowering trees in spring
- Folded paper prayers on bushes
- Multiple images of Jizo
- Gifts of toys and windmills

INFORMATION

- ✚ J8
- ✉ Shiba Koen, Minato-ku. (Lies across the street below Tokyo Tower)
- 🕐 Sunrise–sunset
- 🚇 Onarimon, Shiba-koen
- ♿ Few
- 💴 Free
- ↔ Tokyo Tower (► 34)

Little statues of Jizo are dressed in red baby bonnets

35

11

IMPERIAL PALACE EAST GARDEN

HIGHLIGHTS

- Otemon (gate)
- Flowering cherry trees
- Sculpted hedges
- Monumental stonework
- Base of old castle keep
- Museum of the imperial collections
- Waterbirds
- Giant carp surviving in polluted moat
- Yells of martial arts students

INFORMATION

- J5
- Chiyoda-ku
- 9–4 (no entry after 3PM). Closed Mon, Fri, and Dec 25–Jan 5
- Otemachi, Takebashi
- Tokyo
- Few
- Free
- Museum of Modern Art (► 37)
- More of Imperial Palace grounds can be seen by special permission. For information ☎ 3213–1111 ext 485. Tickets must be collected day before visit. Passports required. Tour times: 10–11:30AM, 1:30–4PM

This was once part of the emperor's private garden. A stone's throw away from the banks and offices of the financial district, it's a haven of peace far from the bustle of the city.

Gateway The Imperial Palace East Garden (Kokyo Higashi Gyoen) is a vast green space in the heart of the city. It was once the biggest fortress in the world, the *shogun*'s castle of Edo, which after 1868 became the site of the Imperial Palace. The East Garden is only a fraction of the whole, but is still big enough for a long walk. The usual entrance is through the Otemon, near the Palace Hotel; it was the main castle gate, one of 36 in the outer walls, and elaborately designed for defense. If you think you hear the ghosts of warring *samurai* shouting, it's probably the police martial arts class in the hall next to the guard house. A small museum near the gate shows exhibits from the imperial collections.

The sights A short walk brings you to the massive foundations of the castle keep, crowning a low hill. Notice the perfect fit of the huge stones in the walls: even the Incas would have been proud of them. There's a good view over the gardens and the city from the top, but imagine—there was once a tower here standing five stories high, and the whole hill was densely packed with buildings. The tower was destroyed by fire in 1657, and most of the remaining buildings were razed after the Meiji restoration of 1868. The gardens are beautifully tended, and there is always something in bloom, notably the azaleas and cherry blossoms in spring and the irises in summer. Huge carp somehow survive in the uninviting waters of the moats, and cormorants perch in wait for smaller fry.

NATIONAL MUSEUM OF MODERN ART

This is the place to see the best of 20th–century painting by Japanese artists, many of them influenced by Western styles. Here their creations are exhibited side by side with major works by their European contemporaries.

The museum The National Museum of Modern Art (Kokuritsu Kindai Bijutsukan) is in Kitanomaru Park, formerly a part of the Imperial Palace gardens. The severe concrete box of a building was designed by Yoshiro Taniguchi and built in 1969. Inside, the galleries are spacious and skillfully lit. The first (ground) floor is used for temporary exhibitions, the top three for the permanent collection. Foreign visitors' eyes will probably be drawn first to the familiar work of Klee, Chagall, and the fine portrait of Alma Mahler by Kokoschka, and then by that of Japanese painters who worked in France and Germany early in the 20th century. Tetsugoro Yorozu's nudes might almost be by Matisse, and Tsuguharu Fujita was practically an honorary Frenchman. But some of the most ravishing pictures are by those who developed the Japanese idiom in new ways, such as Kanzan Shimomura's luminous *Autumn Among Trees*, Gyokudo Kawai's 12-panel *Parting Spring*, and Shinsui Ito's *Snowy Evening*.

Crafts gallery Just across Kitanomaru Park is an impressive brick building—once headquarters of the Imperial Guard. It now houses exhibitions of 20th-century craft work. Fine textiles, graphic design, ceramics, lacquer-work, and metal-work, both traditional and modern, are featured.

HIGHLIGHTS

- *Ascension*, Tatsuoki Nambata
- *Portrait of Alma Mahler*, Kokoschka
- *Deep Woods*, Keigetsu Matsubayashi
- *Bathing*, Taketaro Shinkai
- *Stream*, bronze nude by Taimu Tatahata

INFORMATION

- ✚ J4
- ✉ 3 Kitanomaru Koen, Chiyoda-ku
- ☎ 3214–2561
- 🕐 Tue–Sun 10–5; Fri (in summer) 10–8. Closed Mon (Tue if Mon a national holiday)
- 🚇 Takebashi
- ♿ Good
- 💴 Moderate
- ↔ Imperial Palace East Garden (➤ 36)

Nude Beauty, *Tetsugoro Yorozu*

YASUKUNI SHRINE (YASUKUNI-JINJA)

HIGHLIGHTS

- Steel *torii* weighing 100 tons
- Flocks of white doves
- Japanese garden and flowering trees
- *Samurai* armor and weapons
- Carrier-borne aircraft "Judy"
- Man-guided torpedo
- Oka, rocket plane replica
- Tributes to fallen heroes
- Historic newsreels
- Recording of the emperor's 1945 surrender speech

INFORMATION

- ✚ H4
- ✉ 3-1-1 Kudankita, Chiyoda-ku
- ☎ Museum: 3261–8326
- 🕐 Shrine: daily sunrise–sunset. Museum: Oct–Feb daily 9–4:30. Mar–Sep daily 9–5. Closed Jun 22–23, Dec 28–31
- 🍴 Drinks stand
- 🚇 Kudanshita (Exit 1)
- ♿ Good
- 💰 Shrine: free. Museum: moderate

Every nation honors its war dead, but the War Memorial Museum (Yushukan) still comes as a disturbing surprise to most foreign visitors, and not all Japanese are comfortable about it. The suicide plane and torpedo are chilling relics.

The shrine This Shinto shrine on Kudan Hill, northwest of the Imperial Palace, was founded on the orders of Emperor Meiji in 1869 for the worship of the spirits of those who had sacrificed their lives in the battles for the restoration the previous year. Now it similarly and controversially honors the two-and-a-half million who died "in the defense of the empire" in the years that followed. Since these deaths mainly occurred in what others regard as aggressive wars in China, the Pacific, and Southeast Asia, the term "defense" might seem inappropriate.

The museum The conflicts commemorated include the Russo-Japanese War of 1905, the invasion of Manchuria, and World War II. Exhibits span the change from *samurai* armor and swords to 20th-century guns, tanks, and planes, including a replica Oka, a *kamikaze* rocket-powered winged bomb, and a carrier-borne bomber. Newsreels of the last days of World War II show fleets of B-29s showering bombs on Japan, *kamikaze* pilots taking off on their one-way missions, the devastation caused by the atomic bombs, and the emperor's surrender speech in August 1945.

An entrance to Yasukuni Shrine

NATIONAL DIET BUILDING

This neoclassical blockhouse capped by a stepped pyramid is not beautiful, though the interior is opulent. Sessions viewed from the public gallery or on closed circuit TV can be as lively, or as tedious, as those of any other legislature.

The building A competition was held in 1918 for designs for a new Imperial Diet Building (Kokkaigijido), and work started in 1920. It took 16 years to finish. The slow progress had a lot to do with the growth of Japanese militarism. The last thing the generals who controlled the government had in mind was a genuine parliament. The original architect, Julia Morgan, who built San Simeon in California for William Randolph Hearst, withdrew in the face of constant interference. When the odd-looking building finally opened, the Imperial Diet was no more than a rubber stamp. Not until 1946 was there a general election with universal suffrage, with women voting for the first time. The following year the new National Diet met, replacing the old Imperial Diet.

Visits It is possible to sit in the public gallery of either house when the Diet meets. Foreigners need their passports and, for some sessions, a letter of introduction from their embassy. Admission is by token obtained at the office on the north side of the building. Riots in the Diet are not unknown, but proceedings are rarely so exciting—you can judge from the TV screen in the entrance hall. Most speakers read from prepared scripts which only address contentious issues in the vaguest of terms. When the Diet is not in session, organized tours take you into the 491-member House of Representatives, the 252-member House of Councillors (like a senate), and a selection of other rooms.

HIGHLIGHTS

- Marble halls and bronze doors
- House of Councillors
- Imperial throne
- House of Representatives
- Public gallery
- Stained-glass ceilings
- Emperor's Room
- Lacquer and mother-of-pearl decoration
- Avenue of gingko trees, golden in the fall

INFORMATION

- ✚ H6
- ✉ Chiyoda-ku
- ☎ Upper house: 3581–5111. Lower house: 3581–3111
- ◷ Daily 10–4:30. Closed Mon, national holidays, and Dec 27–Jan 3
- 🍴 Snack bar
- Ⓐ Kokkaigijido-mae, Nagatacho
- ♿ Good
- 🎫 Free
- ↔ Hie Jinja shrine (► 56)
- ❓ Guided tours of the building when the Diet is not in session. Carry your passport

15

HIBIYA PARK

HIGHLIGHTS

- Bonsai shops
- Ponds and fountains
- Floral borders, even in winter
- Outdoor auditorium concerts
- Imperial Hotel, opposite
- Intricate supports for precious trees
- Hibiya City—winter skating

INFORMATION

- ✚ J6
- ✉ Chiyoda-ku
- 🕓 Dawn–11PM
- 🍴 Good restaurant and snack bars
- Ⓜ Hibiya, Uchisaiwaicho
- 🚃 Yurakucho
- ♿ Good
- 🎫 Free
- ↔ Ginza (➤ 41), Idemitsu Museum of Arts (➤ 52)

Chrysanthemums are highly prized in Japan

This island of tranquillity is one of Tokyo's escape valves. Lovers find a private corner, secretaries from nearby offices come to eat their box lunches, and tired tourists can rest from sightseeing.

The park The city's first public park adds a green extension to the huge open space of the Imperial Palace Outer Garden. The ministry buildings of Kasumigaseki line one side and the edge of Ginza is only a block away on the other. In the park itself fountains play, waterbirds swim on the ponds, and gardeners groom the impeccable flowerbeds and trim the trees. The constructions of rope and wood they build to support precious specimens through the winter are works of art. Facilities include public tennis courts, a restaurant, a shop selling perfect little bonsai trees, and an outdoor auditorium for occasional pop and rock concerts on weekend afternoons. But people mostly come to stroll and sit, away from crowds and traffic. It's a favorite with visitors from out of town, too, who always seem to want to be photographed here.

The vicinity Facing the southeast side of the park is the massive Imperial Hotel (1970), which replaced Frank Lloyd Wright's 1920s hotel when that was deemed too small and difficult to maintain and was torn down in 1967. The new hotel's vast lobby is one of Tokyo's favorite meeting points. Nearby Hibiya City is modeled after New York's Rockefeller Plaza, with part of it flooded and frozen into an outdoor skating-rink in winter. Across the Harumi-dori from the Imperial Hotel is the Dai-Ichi building—once General MacArthur's headquarters.

GINZA

Everyone seems to have heard about Ginza, the most expensive real estate on earth, and its shops and clubs with prices to match. But there's no need to spend a fortune. There are places to suit modest budgets—and looking costs you nothing.

Shops The name Ginza comes from the silver mint which the *shogun* built in the area in 1612. Money attracts money, and merchants soon set up shop nearby. Their successors are the famous department stores of today, two of which—Wako and Mitsukoshi—stand at the heart of Ginza, the "Yon-chome" (4-chome) crossing. This is where the two main streets meet, Harumi-dori and Chuo-dori. The latter is transformed on Sunday afternoons into a pedestrian precinct. If the weather is fine, cafés put out tables and sunshades. The shopping is not all on a grand scale. Down the side streets, you can find boutiques and little discount stores where prices are almost reasonable, as well as hostess clubs and bars where they are outrageous. Restaurants can be extraordinarily expensive too, but you will usually find somewhere to eat that is sensibly priced at one of the department stores (➤ 73, panel).

Sights The wide, straight streets of Ginza date from 1872, when a fire destroyed much of the area. In spite of the steel-and-glass look and the neon signs, several late 19th-century buildings survive, including the Wako store with a famous clock tower, a landmark and a favorite meeting point. Down Harumi-dori near Higashi-Ginza subway station is the rebuilt Kabuki-za Theater, with matinée and evening performances on most days. Continue in the same direction and you will reach Tsukiji Fish Market and the Sumida River.

HIGHLIGHTS

- Ginza 4-chome crossing
- Lights of Ginza by night
- Wako's elegant displays
- Shoppers in designer clothing
- Basement food departments
- Mikimoto pearl shop
- Kabuki-za Theater
- Beer halls
- Side street discount shops
- Sunday strolling on Chuo-dori

INFORMATION

- ✚ K6/7
- ✉ Chuo-ku
- ◷ 24 hours
- 🍴 Countless restaurants and fast-food outlets
- Ⓢ Ginza, Higashi-Ginza
- 🚉 Yurakucho
- ♿ Few
- 🆓 Free
- ↔ Hibiya Park (➤ 40), Sony Center (➤ 42), Tsukiji Fish Market (➤ 44), Idemitsu Museum of Arts (➤ 52), Kabuki-za Theater (➤ 78)

SONY CENTER

HIGHLIGHTS

- Super-realistic video games
- Big screen HDTV
- Make your own video
- Tiny walkmans and VCRs
- Minidisc
- Digital cameras
- Global positioning
- 3D TV
- Laser disc movie shows
- Transparent-cased equipment

INFORMATION

🔢 K6

✉ 5-3-1 Ginza, Chuo-ku

☎ 3573–2371

🕐 11–7

🍴 Cafés on several levels; restaurants in same building

🚇 Ginza

🚇 Yurakucho

♿ Few

🎟 Free

↔ Ginza (► 41)

The Sony Plaza

Here are seven floors with electronic marvels set up for hands-on testing, including some devices that will not have reached your home market yet. There's always a line of people waiting to play the latest video games.

Showroom Japan leads the world in consumer electronics, launching an endless succession of innovations. Sony—one of the biggest companies, and the one that put "walkman" into the world's dictionaries—is in the forefront, and this center in Ginza is its shop window. Here you can not only see but try out the new products. If you haven't yet caught up with laser discs or digital cameras, this is your chance. Miniaturization is a specialty, with tiny cellular phones, personal CD players, minicams, and videos. Positioning equipment using earth satellites was top secret not so many years ago; now there are simple hand-held models that will tell you accurately where on earth you are and mark the spot on a map.

Demonstrations When everyone has a television, industry has to produce something better and the marketing wizards have to persuade people to buy it. High definition television (HDTV) is already here; you can see its brilliantly crisp pictures on a huge screen. Next on the market may be three-dimensional TV and then, no doubt, holographic images you can walk right around and through; both systems are demonstrated. Some of the most intriguing exhibits are the working examples of consumer electronics encased in transparent bodies so you can see what's inside. If you need a break, you'll find cafés on alternate floors.

HAMA RIKYU GARDEN

The scene can have changed little since feudal lords came duck hunting here. Note the contrast between the organized chaos of Tsukiji Market right next door and this haven of tranquillity.

The garden Now hemmed in between an expressway and the Sumida River, the Hama Rikyu Garden (Hama Detached Palace Garden), comprising 62 acres of water, woods, and gardens, was once part of the private game reserve of the Tokugawa *shogun*s. It came into the hands of the imperial family in 1871 and was given to the city in 1945. Clever planting ensures that some species are always in bloom, and big areas are much less "tamed" and formal than in the typical Japanese garden. The ponds are still planted thickly with reeds and bamboo to provide cover for hundreds of ducks and other waterbirds. The river is tidal this close to its mouth, and seawater flows in and out of one of the ponds. Long causeway bridges with wisteria-covered trellises lead across the river to a replica of the picturesque Nakajima teahouse where Emperor Meiji entertained President Ulysses S. Grant and Mrs. Grant in 1879. A 300-year-old pine tree near the entrance was planted by one of the early *shogun*s.

River boat Apart from the pleasure of strolling in the garden, the best reason for a visit is to catch one of the frequent water buses for a cruise upriver to Asakusa. The terminal is at the eastern tip of the garden, a seven-minute walk from the entrance, though you'll want to take longer. Boats leave every half-hour or so, and the trip takes 45 minutes. You couldn't call it beautiful, but the river has been cleaned up a lot, with landscaped gardens along its banks, and it's certainly a different view of Tokyo.

HIGHLIGHTS

- River views
- Duck lakes, once used for hunting
- Seawater tidal pond
- Causeway bridges
- Teahouse
- Japanese formal garden
- Peony garden
- Flowering trees, all year
- Precious trees wrapped up for winter
- River cruises

INFORMATION

- ✛ K8
- ✉ 1-1 Hamarikyuteien, Chuo-ku
- ☎ 3541–0200
- 🕐 Tue–Sun 9–4:30. Closed Mon, and Dec 29–Jan 3
- Ⓣ Shinbashi, Higashi-Ginza
- ♿ Few
- 🍴 Moderate
- ↔ Tsukiji Fish Market (➤ 44)

TSUKIJI FISH MARKET

INFORMATION

- ✠ K/L7–8
- ✉ Tsukiji, Chuo-ku
- ☎ 3542–1111
- 🕐 Mon–Sat 5AM–3PM. Closed Sun, national holidays, and market holidays (check at tourist offices)
- 🍴 Superb *sushi* bars and many noodle stalls
- Ⓣ Tsukiji, Higashi-Ginza
- ♿ Free
- ⬌ Ginza (➤ 41), Hama Rikyu Garden (➤ 43)

Set your alarm clock for 4AM and catch the first subway train to Tsukiji Station. The effort of getting out of bed at such an unearthly hour is repaid by Tokyo's most amazing spectacle, the pre-dawn tuna auctions.

The auctions The Japanese believe the best way of cooking fish is not to cook it at all, so it has to reach the consumer in perfect condition. An enormous industry ensures that it does, and 90 percent of the fish eaten in Tokyo passes through Tsukiji Fish Market in the Central Wholesale Market. The action begins at 5AM with buyers inspecting the giant bluefin tuna, smaller yellowfin, and aptly named "bigeyes," flown in fresh from all over the world. The auctioneer rings a handbell and in seconds the first fish are sold—some for a price that would buy a small car.

The market In the neighboring wholesale market, 1,200 stalls sell every sort of fish and crustacean, most of them still jumping or crawling. As struggling masses of them are poured from one container to another, water cascades onto the floor and into the shoes of the unwary (so wear boots or tie some plastic bags over your footwear). Buyers for the city's many restaurants and shops crowd the narrow alleys, so make a getaway to one of the nearby *sushi* bars (➤ 66) for a Japanese breakfast.

A market trader prepares her stall in Tsukiji Fish Market

TOKYO STOCK EXCHANGE

You see the action on the live trading floor as well as in the computer rooms where financial wizards commune with their screens in complete silence and move unimaginable sums of money around the world.

Visits The Tokyo Exchange outgrew its old building in the postwar boom, and when this new granite fortress was opened in 1984 a lot of attention was paid to educating and entertaining visitors. Time your visit to coincide with trading hours on the floor of the exchange, from 9 to 11, or 12:30 to 3. A bell sounds the opening and closing; in between, keen young men wave to get attention and then semaphore their bids or offers, although most trading is done on screens these days. A shiny metal robot in the second-floor public gallery demonstrates some of the hand signals: holding an imaginary telephone to the ear means NTT; holding the nose means Tokyo Gas! Another robot in the shape of an eccentric professor explains the workings of the market, while multilingual earphones dispense still more information. Upstairs in the silent computer trading rooms the atmosphere could not be more different from the busy trading floor. Here the dealers buy and sell futures and options with a mere tap at their keyboards.

Local shrine Outside the Stock Exchange, look for the little Kabuto-jinja, a shrine almost opposite the main door with a double-deck expressway right overhead. Supposedly marking the site where an 11th-century warrior buried a golden helmet as a thanks-offering for victory, the shrine gave its name to this part of Tokyo—Kabuto-cho—and, by association, to the world of Japanese investment, like "Wall Street" in New York or "the City" in London.

HIGHLIGHTS

- Exhibition plaza
- View of trading floor
- Hand signal robot
- Lessons in "How to Trade"
- Multilingual explanations
- 3D screens
- Computer trading rooms
- Museum
- Kabuto shrine

INFORMATION

- L5
- 2-1 Nihonbashi-kabutocho, Chuo-ku
- 3665–1881
- Mon–Fri 9–4. Closed Sat, Sun, and national holidays
- Many good eating places nearby
- Nihonbashi
- Tokyo (10 minutes' walk)
- Very good
- Free
- Bridgestone Museum of Art (➤ 52), Yamatane Museum of Art (➤ 53)

TOKYO NATIONAL MUSEUM

HIGHLIGHTS

- Jomon-era clay masks
- 3rd-century BC bronze bells
- Terra-cotta burial figures
- Decorative tiles
- Imari ware
- Noh costumes, 16th–18th centuries
- 1664 palanquin
- Sword collection
- Han Dynasty stone reliefs
- Tang Dynasty horses and camel

INFORMATION

- L1
- Ueno Park, Taito-ku
- 3822–1111
- Tue–Sun 9–4:30. Closed Mon (Tue if Mon a national holiday), and Dec 26–Jan 3
- A small restaurant serves snacks and light meals
- Ueno
- Ueno
- Good
- Moderate
- National Museum of Western Art (➤ 47), Shitamachi Museum (➤ 48)

A great museum—and this is one—compels your interest in fields you have never before thought about. Every aspect of Japanese art and archaeology is here combined with a fine collection of other Asian art, and the quality of the exhibits is breathtaking.

Archaeology The smallest of the three main buildings of the Tokyo National Museum (Tokyo Kokuritsu Hakubutsukan), the Hyokeikan, is on the left as you face the museum entrance. It houses relics found in archaeological digs all over Japan: prehistoric flint axes, elaborate pottery from around 3000BC, bronze bells and sword blades. Many intriguing terra-cotta burial figures—musicians, horses, and wild boars—date from the 3rd to 6th centuries.

The Japanese collection The central Honkan building displays the finest of Japanese art: not only painting and sculpture, but calligraphy, *ukiyo-e* (woodblock prints; ➤ 53, panel), ceramics including the celebrated Imari ware, swords, and armor. There are exquisite Noh theater costumes, some of which date from the 16th century. English explanations are limited mainly to names and dates.

Other Asian art The third and newest building, the Toyokan, is the most surprising, and the collections are the best displayed. The Chinese exhibits include jade and bronzes, 1st-century stone reliefs, Tang Dynasty ceramic horses and a camel, precious porcelain, and textiles. Korea, Southeast Asia, Iran, Iraq, and even Ancient Egypt are represented. Gondara Buddhist sculpture from Central Asia shows the influence of ancient Greek art during and after the time of Alexander the Great.

NATIONAL MUSEUM OF WESTERN ART

You may not have come to Tokyo with the idea of seeing masterpieces of European art, but this collection, mainly formed by one visionary in the early 20th century, is too good to miss.

The museum The National Museum of Western Art (Kokuritsu Seiyo Bijutsukan) is on the right of the main gate to Ueno Park from the JR station. A typically uncompromising concrete building, it was designed by Le Corbusier to hold the art collection of Kojiro Matsukata. Matsukata was a successful businessman who spent a lot of time in Europe in the early years of the 20th century and developed a passion for the work of the French Impressionists. His collection eventually numbered hundreds of works, including some of the finest paintings by Monet, Renoir, Gauguin (the pre-Tahiti period), and Van Gogh, and over 50 of the most famous Rodin bronzes (including *The Thinker* and *The Burghers of Calais*). Matsukata kept them in Europe, but after World War II they were brought to Japan and bequeathed to the nation in his will. The museum was opened in 1959.

The growing collection Kojiro Matsukata's inspired acquisitions are still its greatest strength, but for a museum of Western art there was a need to broaden the scope beyond one era and one country. Many major purchases have been made in recent years. At one end of the time scale there are old masters, including works by Tintoretto, Rubens, and El Greco, while at the other the moderns range from Max Ernst to Jackson Pollock. You can stroll among the sculptures in the museum's courtyard; inside, good lighting does justice to some wonderful paintings.

HIGHLIGHTS

- *Crucifixion*, El Greco
- *Summer Evening Landscape in Italy*, Claude-Joseph Vernet
- *The Loving Cup*, D. G. Rossetti
- Rodin bronzes
- *Landscape of Brittany*, Gauguin
- *On the Boat*, Monet
- *Water Lilies*, Monet
- *Parisiennes in Algerian Costume*, Renoir
- *The Port of St. Tropez*, Signac
- *The Petrified Forest*, Ernst

INFORMATION

- L2
- Ueno Park, Taito-ku
- 3828–5131
- Tue–Sun 9:30–5. Closed Mon (Tue if Mon a national holiday), and Dec 26– Jan 3
- Drinks stand; snacks outside
- Ueno
- Ueno (Park exit)
- Good
- Expensive
- Tokyo National Museum (➤ 46), Shitamachi Museum (➤ 48)

Above: Rodin's The Burghers of Calais *in the museum courtyard*

23

SHITAMACHI MUSEUM

HIGHLIGHTS

- Children's games and toys
- Evocative early photographs
- Merchant's shop-house
- Candy shop and house
- Coppersmith's workshop
- Shrine and fortune-telling box
- *Haiku* poet's room
- *Hanao* (sandal strap) maker at work
- Old rickshaws
- Recorded street cries

INFORMATION

- ✚ L2
- ✉ 2-1 Ueno Koen, Taito-ku
- ☎ 3823–7451
- 🕐 Tue–Sun 9:30–4:30. Closed Mon (Tue if Mon a national holiday), and Dec 29–Jan 3
- 🍴 Small coffee shop; snack bars and restaurants nearby
- 🚇 Ueno, Ueno-hirokoji, Yushima
- 🚉 Ueno
- ♿ Few
- 💷 Inexpensive
- ↔ Tokyo National Museum (➤ 46), National Museum of Western Art (➤ 47), Ueno Park (➤ 59)

This compact and charming record of the old working-class parts of the city conveys a real sense of the way people lived a century ago; and you can handle many everyday objects of the past, forgotten in the rush to modernize.

A different museum Facing the southeast corner of the Shinobazu Pond in Ueno Park is an unassuming building, with only an old-fashioned red mailbox to suggest that it is unusual. Inside, a fairly small space has been turned into crooked streets of shops and houses, packed together just the way they were in this part of the city before fire and the bulldozers swept them away. Tiny rooms are equipped with items contributed by people still living in the area, simple furniture and utensils that fell out of use almost unnoticed when labor-saving devices made them redundant. In one house, notice the bamboo basket with a long pole to carry away valuables in case of a fire, a perennial hazard in the old wooden city.

Hands on This is no ordinary museum. The enthusiastic people who run it really want you to get your hands on the exhibits, and some speak quite good English. Children can play with traditional games and toys, and craftspeople are sometimes on hand to demonstrate old skills: strap-weaving, sandal-making, even how to wash clothes in a tub, using a washboard to get them clean. There's a tiny bath house, with separate entrances for men and women, and a coffeehouse with an ancient gramophone, complete with huge trumpet. Recordings of street cries are played, and early photographs depict the people who might have made them as well as all sorts of surprising details of everyday life.

Above: everyday tools and equipment were donated by local people

ASAKUSA KANNON TEMPLE

Old Japan lives on in the friendly Asakusa quarter. Its temple has more colorful ceremonies than any other in Tokyo, but even when nothing much is happening there's a happy crowd here. Visit once and you'll want to come again.

The people's favorite The Asakusa Kannon Temple (Sensoji Temple) has its origins in the 7th century and was later dedicated to uniting the competing Buddhist factions. Pilgrims came from all over Japan, and Asakusa set about entertaining them—providing food and lodging, theaters, *onsen* (baths), and houses of pleasure. Leveled by earthquakes, bombs, and fires, it was always rebuilt much the same as before and remains the favorite haunt of out-of-town visitors and the foreigners who discover it. Late afternoon is a good time to come, when dozens of food stalls start cooking and circus performers amuse the crowds.

The sights Near the subway station, opposite the Kaminarimon gate to the temple precinct, it's worth calling at the local information center for maps and leaflets. Through the gate is Nakamise-dori, a pedestrian street lined by little shops, which leads to a second gate, Hozomon, with an elegant five-story pagoda. Straight ahead lies the main shrine hall, just beyond a great bronze urn wreathed in incense smoke, which visitors wave over themselves to benefit from its curative properties. To the right is Asakusa Jinja, a Shinto shrine. The east gate, Nitenmon, survives largely intact from the year 1618.

HIGHLIGHTS

- Nakamise-dori: little shops
- Hozomon (gate)
- Five-story pagoda
- Worshippers "washing" in smoke
- Main Sensoji Shrine
- Tokinokane Bell
- Denbo-in Temple Garden (► 58)
- Chingodo Temple
- Rice-cracker makers
- Clowns and acrobats

INFORMATION

- ✚ N2
- ✉ 2-3-1 Asakusa, Taito-ku
- ☎ 3842–0181
- 🕐 6AM–sunset
- 🍴 The area is noted for good restaurants
- Ⓢ Asakusa
- ♿ Good
- ✋ Free
- ⬌ Sumida River cruise (► 43), Kappabashi (► 61)
- ❓ Included in many city tours

A bronze Buddha in the temple gardens

TOKYO DISNEYLAND

INFORMATION

- ✚ Off map
- ✉ 1-1 Maihama, Urayasu-shi
- ☎ 0473/54–0001 (recording in Japanese only)
- 🕐 Open 9AM. Closing time varies from 7 to 10PM. Closed six days in mid-Jan
- 🍴 Many restaurants and snack bars
- 🚉 Urayasu, then bus
- 🚆 Maihama, (15 minutes from Tokyo Station via Keiyo Line), then free shuttle bus to Disneyland or to the hotel area
- ♿ Very good
- 💰 Expensive
- ❓ Tour companies offer day trips from Tokyo. 40 minutes by shuttle bus from Narita International Airport, Tokyo Station (Yaesu north exit) or Ueno Station (Iriya exit)

The plummet from the summit of Splash Mountain

Only the Japanese could run an even cleaner, keener Disneyland than the Disney organization itself. The visitors are part of the show and they're having a wonderful time, even if they scream less than Americans on Space Mountain.

The park A near replica of the California original, although slightly bigger, the Tokyo version is owned and operated under license by a local company set up by big banks and industrial corporations. It opened in 1983 and was an instant success, with over 10 million visitors in the first year. All the most popular rides and attractions found in other Disney parks are here too. On busy days—mainly weekends and holidays—you may have to stand in line for half an hour for Splash Mountain, Space Mountain, or Star Tours. Midweek, there may be no wait at all. The "cast members" (staff) are utterly committed: see the cleaners' high-speed ballet as they whisk up any trace of litter. And where else do they bow as you board the rides and again when you get off? It isn't the Japanese way to walk around and eat at the same time, so there are fewer snack places than in the US parks.

Staying over The five big resort hotels clustered close to Disneyland are all packed with families every weekend, but being near the city and on the way to the airport, they are popular business venues as well.

TOKYO's *best*

ART COLLECTIONS

See Top 25 Sights for
NATIONAL MUSEUM OF MODERN ART (▶ 37)
NATIONAL MUSEUM OF WESTERN ART (▶ 47)

Bridgestone highlights

- *Mlle Georgette Charpentier Seated*, Renoir
- *Saltimbanque Seated with Arms Crossed*, Picasso
- *Windmills on Montmartre*, Van Gogh
- *Self-portrait*, Manet
- *Mont Sainte-Victoire and Château Noir*, Cézanne
- *Still Life with Cat*, Tsuguharu Fujita
- Japanese Post-Impressionists
- *Faunesse*, Rodin
- Degas bronzes
- *Desire*, Maillol

Toshusai Sharaku's Sawamura Sojuro III in the Role of Kujaku Saburo *in the Ota Memorial Museum of Art*

BRIDGESTONE MUSEUM OF ART (BRIDGESTONE BIJUTSUKAN)

The founder of the Bridgestone Tire Company, Shojiro Ishibashi (a play on his name, *ishibashi*, means "stone bridge"), used some of his wealth to buy art. He specialized in the French Impressionists and Post-Impressionists, and Meiji-period Japanese artists who painted in a Western style. A sculpture collection includes ancient Egyptian, Greek, and Roman, as well as 20th-century, works.

➕ L6 ✉ 1-10-1, Kyobashi, Chuo-ku (entrance on Yaesu-dori) ☎ 3563–0241 ◷ Tue–Sun 10–5.30. Closed Mon, late Dec–early Jan, and weeks before and after special exhibitions 🍴 Cafés and restaurants nearby 🚇 Kyobashi, Nihonbashi ✋ Moderate

IDEMITSU MUSEUM OF ARTS (IDEMITSU BIJUTSUKAN)

Superb Asian art includes calligraphy, painting, and ceramics. Two 16th-century screens—one of cherry blossoms, the other of golden autumn leaves—show that Japanese reverence for these subjects is nothing new. The collection, formed by oil industry magnate Sazo Idemitsu (1885–1981), is so vast that only a tiny fraction can be shown at one time. One room is devoted to the odd but fascinating archive of potsherds of the world. View central Tokyo from the museum's windows.

➕ K6 ✉ Kokusai (International) Building (9F), 3-1-1 Marunouchi, Chiyoda-ku ☎ 3213–9402 ◷ Tue–Sun 10–5. Closed Mon, and Dec 29–Jan 3 🍴 Coffee bar 🚇 Yurakucho ✋ Moderate

NEZU INSTITUTE OF FINE ARTS (NEZU BIJUTSUKAN)

This treasury of Japanese and other oriental fine arts is set in its own beautiful gardens, dotted with tea ceremony pavilions.

➕ F8 ✉ 6-5-1 Minami-Aoyama, Minato-ku ☎ 3400–2536 ◷ Tue–Sun 9:30–4:30. Closed Mon and day after national holidays 🍴 Nearby snack bar and restaurants 🚇 Omotesando (10 minutes' walk) ✋ Expensive

OTA MEMORIAL MUSEUM OF ART (UKIYO-E OTA KINEN BIJUTSUKAN)

In a side street off Omotesando-dori, this museum is a complete contrast to the modern fashion street scene outside. You have to exchange your shoes for slippers, and even these must be discarded before you approach some of the showcases. The *ukiyo-e* prints (see panel opposite), and the original paintings from which they were made, were collected by business magnate Seizo Ota (1893–1977). He amassed 10,000, and the museum has acquired more, so the displays are frequently rotated.

🔲 E7 ✉ 1-10-10 Jingumae, Shibuya ku ☎ 3403 0880 🕐 Tue–Sun 10:30–5:30. Closed Mon, from 26th to end of each month, and Dec 19–Jan 2 🍴 Drinks and snacks in basement 🚇 Meijijingu-mae 🚉 Harajuku (JR) 💰 Moderate

SEIJI TOGO MEMORIAL ART MUSEUM

Many of the paintings on show here are by Seiji Togo (1897–1978), whose work depicts Japanese feminine grace and beauty. The museum made headlines when it paid a world record price for Van Gogh's *Sunflowers*, and it is also noted for its 33 pictures by the American primitive, Grandma Moses.

🔲 D4 ✉ Yasuda Kasai Kaijo Building 42F, 1-26-1 Nishi-Shinjuku, Shinjuku-ku ☎ 3349–3081 🕐 Tue–Sun 9:30–4:30. Closed Mon, and Dec 27–Jan 4 🍴 Restaurants in same building 🚇 Shinjuku 💰 Moderate

A ceramic dish in the collection of the Suntory Museum

SUNTORY MUSEUM

The famous whiskey company is a great patron of the arts. This museum houses a small but beautiful display of some of the best of Japanese traditional art in rotating exhibitions of paintings, ceramics, lacquerware, textiles, and carvings.

🔲 G6 ✉ Suntory Building 11F, 1-2-3 Moto-Akasaka, Minato-ku ☎ 3470–1073 🕐 Tue–Thu, Sat–Sun 10–4:30; Fri 10–1. Closed Mon 🍴 Teahouse. Restaurants in same building 🚇 Akasakamitsuke 💰 Moderate

TOKYO METROPOLITAN FINE ART GALLERY

The spacious galleries accommodate touring exhibitions and modern art shows. There is also a small permanent collection of 20th-century Japanese art, mostly in Western styles. The café is a good spot to rest from your museum-touring.

🔲 L1 ✉ Ueno Park, Taito-ku ☎ 3821–3726 🕐 Tue–Sun 9–4. Closed Mon 🍴 Café 🚇 Ueno 💰 Free (except special exhibitions)

YAMATANE MUSEUM OF ART (YAMATANE BIJUTSUKAN)

This museum occupies two floors of an office building in the heart of Tokyo's business district. The collection features paintings by the best Japanese artists working in the traditional style, mostly from the post-1868 Meiji period. Trees, birds, and Mount Fuji are recurring themes. Visit the museum shop.

🔲 L5 ✉ Yamatane Building 8/9F, 7-12 Nihonbashi-kabutocho, Chuo-ku ☎ 3669–7643 🕐 Tue–Sun 10–5. Closed Mon, national holidays, and Dec 28–Jan 3 🚇 Nihonbashi 💰 Expensive

Ukiyo-e

Woodblock prints (*ukiyo-e*) were art for the common people, depicting views, beautiful women, and *kabuki* actors. They were highly popular from about 1700, and new designs are still being produced today. Katsushika Hokusai (1760–1849), painter of *The 36 Views of Mount Fuji*, and Utagawa Hiroshige (1797–1858) are among the greatest names, well known internationally. Early prints in fine condition are worth fortunes, and even modern hand-colored copies can be expensive. These days, color-laser copies make a convincing substitute.

MUSEUMS

Trains and boats and planes

One of the locomotives in front of the Transportation Museum was built in the United States in 1880, the other in England in 1881. Preserved inside is the oldest of all, built in 1871 at the Vulcan works, Newton le Willows, England. It pulled Japan's first train the following year.

There are ship models from all eras, and fine model aircraft. The Henri Farman biplane suspended from the roof made the first powered flight in Japan in 1910.

Exhibit in the National Science Museum

JAPAN FOLK CRAFT MUSEUM (NIHON MINGEIKAN)

This collection is a tribute to the beauty of everyday objects of the mainly rural past. The museum was started in the 1920s by Yanagi Soetsu, one of the founders of the Japanese Arts and Crafts movement. The building itself is a replica of an old rural farmhouse.

🚇 B8 ✉ 4-3-33 Komaba, Meguro-ku ☎ 3467–4527 🕐 Tue–Sun 10–5. Closed Mon, and Dec 26–Jan 3 🍴 Snacks 🚉 Komabatodai-mae (Inokashira Line) 💲 Moderate

MUSEUM OF MARITIME SCIENCE

A building like a concrete ship, on an island in Tokyo Bay, houses displays on all aspects of ships and sailing. Historic vessels are moored nearby.

🚇 Off map in Tokyo Bay ✉ 3-1 Higashi-Yashio, Shinagawa-ku ☎ 5500–1111 🕐 Mon–Fri 10–5; Sat, Sun, holidays 10–6. Closed Dec 28–31 🍴 Restaurants and snack bar 🚉 Fune-no-kagakukan (from Shinbashi via Yurikamome overhead line) 🚢 River bus from Hinode Pier (🚇 K8) 💲 Moderate

TOKYO METROPOLITAN MUSEUM OF PHOTOGRAPHY

The museum is part of the new Yebisu Garden Place development (➤ 32). Early photographs include some from before the Meiji Restoration of 1868, recording daily life of the time. Imaginative displays demonstrate optical illusions and their modern equivalent, holography.

🚇 E10 ✉ 1-13-3 Mita, Meguro-ku ☎ 3280–0031 🕐 Tue–Thu, Sat–Sun 10–6; Fri 10–9. Closed Mon (Tue if Mon a national holiday), and Dec 28–Jan 4 🍴 Huge beer hall, restaurants, and fast-food outlets all nearby 🚉 Ebisu 💲 Expensive

TRANSPORTATION MUSEUM

From Kanda Station look for a couple of historic locomotives parked outside the museum. Inside, exhibits include a big model railway, the nose of a 747 jet airliner, and a demonstration of magnetic levitation—the frictionless transportation system of the future. Human-powered modes of transportation include a palanquin, a rickshaw, and a trishaw from as late as 1948. Among the historic cars, a quaint 1954 Suzuki and 1958 baby Subaru were the start of something big, the colossal Japanese motor industry.

🚇 K/L4 ✉ 1-25 Kanda-Sudacho, Chiyoda-ku ☎ 3251–8481 🕐 Tue–Sun 9:30–5. Closed Mon, and Dec 29–Jan 3 🍴 Snack bar 🚉 Kanda (Exit 6) 💲 Moderate

VIEWS FROM THE TOP

See Top 25 Sights for
METROPOLITAN GOVERNMENT OFFICES (► 26)
TOKYO TOWER (► 34)

AKASAKA PRINCE
The hotel stands on a central hilltop site, so the bar and restaurant on the top of its 40 stories have the city's best view of Akasaka, the Imperial Palace, Ginza, and Tokyo Bay.
✚ H6 ✉ 1-2 Kioi-cho, Chiyoda-ku ☎ 3234–1111 🕐 Daily 11:30AM–midnight 🍴 Bar and restaurant 🚇 Nagatacho

KEIO PLAZA HOTEL 47TH FLOOR
The rooftop of the first skyscraper to be built in Shinjuku is a spectacular vantage point. At night, the window seats in the hotel's penthouse cocktail bars wouldn't suit sufferers from vertigo, and the prices are similarly elevated.
✚ D4 ✉ 2-2-1 Nishi-Shinjuku, Shinjuku-ku ☎ 3344–0111 🕐 Daily 10–6 🍴 Snacks, plus many restaurants in hotel 🚇 Shinjuku 💰 Moderate

SUMITOMO TOWER
This 52-story, six-sided building with a hollow center has a lookout point, and the top three floors are given over to restaurants used by office workers at lunchtime. Some stay open in the evening. Window tables have the kind of view you might get from a spaceship.
✚ D4 ✉ 2-6-1 Nishi-Shinjuku, Shinjuku-ku 🕐 Daily 9AM–10PM 🍴 Many restaurants 🚇 Shinjuku 💰 Free

SUNSHINE 60 OBSERVATORY
One of the world's fastest elevators carries you to the 60th floor in less than a minute. Choose a clear day: when the smog is bad you can see only the local area— one of Tokyo's ugliest. The same huge complex also houses the Ancient Orient Museum and a planetarium. An aquarium on the 10th floor is home to 20,000 fish of over 600 species, a coral reef, snowy penguin habitat, and outdoor marine garden. The seawater for the tanks is pumped from far out in Tokyo Bay.
✚ Off map ✉ Sunshine City, 3-1-3 Higachi-Ikebukuro, Toshima-ku ☎ 3989–3331 🕐 Jul 21–Aug 31 daily 10–8:30. Sep 1–Jul 20 Mon–Sat 10–6; Sun and national holidays 10–6:30 🍴 Restaurants and snack bars 🚇 Higachi-Ikebukuro 💰 Expensive

WESTIN TOKYO HOTEL
The 22nd-floor bar and restaurant here, and the top of Yebisu in the same complex, look out on the Post-Modern Garden Place (► 32), north to Shibuya, and east to Shingawa and the bay.
✚ E10 ✉ Yebisu Garden Place, 1-4-1 Mita, Meguro-ku ☎ 5423–7000 🕐 Daily 11AM–midnight 🍴 Bar and restaurant 🚇 Ebisu

An aerial view of the skyscrapers of Shinjuku

Ikebukuro
A little off the tourist trail but easy to reach by subway and JR's Yamanote loop between Shinjuku and Ueno is Ikebukuro, one of the city's growth areas. In the middle of a working-class district, big business has planted a few enormous buildings and the city's largest department stores, including a monster Seibu, Tobu, and the amazing Tokyu Hands home improvement store (► 76). Toyota's Amlux showroom (► 60) is across the street from Sunshine 60.

SHRINES & TEMPLES

Shinto

Most Japanese are to some extent followers of Shinto, which they call *Kami-no-Michi*, meaning the "Way of the Gods (or Spirits)". Originating as a belief in the spirits of nature, it places great emphasis on purity of conduct, mind, and motive, and corresponding physical cleanliness. A Shinto shrine (*jinja* or *jingu*) is marked by its *torii* gate or gates, shaped like a giant perch for the mythical cock which crowed and brought the sun goddess Amaterasu out of her cave to light up the world.

Worshippers at Hie Jinja

See Top 25 Sights for
ASAKUSA KANNON (SENSOJI) TEMPLE (► 49)
MEIJI SHRINE (► 30)
SENGAKUJI TEMPLE (► 33)
YASUKUNI SHRINE (► 38)
ZOJOJI TEMPLE (► 35)

HANAZONO SHRINE

Now surrounded by the monuments of commerce and pleasure, this is one of the oldest shrines in Tokyo. People pray here for success in business.
➕ E4 ✉ Opposite Marui Interior store, Shinjuku 3-chome, Shinjuku-ku ⏰ Sunrise–9PM 🍴 Plenty nearby 🚇 Shinjuku San-chome 💲 Free

HIE JINJA

One of Tokyo's most picturesque shrines is opposite the main entrance to the Capitol Tokyu Hotel, up a steep flight of steps. You will notice statues of monkeys carrying their young: one of the deities enshrined here is believed to protect women against miscarriages. Hie Jinja was a favorite of the *shoguns* and the site of Edo's greatest religious festival.
➕ H6 ✉ 2-10-5 Nagatacho, Chiyoda-ku ☎ 3581–2471 ⏰ Sunrise–sunset 🚇 Kokkaigijido-mae 💲 Free

KANDA MYOJIN SHRINE

One of Tokyo's oldest foundations and the focus of the Kanda Festival, held in alternate years in May. The festival's highlight is a procession of dozens of portable shrines. The present shrine buildings are replicas of those destroyed in the earthquake and fires of 1923. On Sundays young couples come to have their weddings blessed, the brides gorgeously arrayed in their most expensive kimonos.
➕ K3 ✉ 2-16-2 Soto-Kanda, Chiyoda-ku ☎ 3254–0753 ⏰ Sunrise–sunset 🚇 Ochanomizu 💲 Free

KIYOMIZU KANNON

Bullet holes in the gate, Kuromon, date from the 1868 battle for the hill. Childless women pray to a Kannon figure in the shrine, and, if they subsequently have a baby, return to leave a doll in gratitude and to pray for the child's good health. Every September 25 the accumulated dolls are burned in a great bonfire.
➕ L2 ✉ Ueno Koen, Taito-ku ⏰ Sunrise–sunset 🍴 Plenty nearby 🚇 Ueno 💲 Free

SOGENJI TEMPLE

Close to the Kappabashi shops (► 61), this is also known as Kappa Temple, a name derived from the legendary water sprites who helped to drain the marshes that once covered this area.
➕ M1 ✉ 3-7-2 Matsugaya, Taito-ku ☎ 3841–2035 ⏰ Sunrise–sunset 🚇 Iriya 💲 Free

SUMIYOSHI SHRINE
Fishermen were brought to this island in the Sumida River from Osaka by Ieyasu Tokugawa to set up a fishing industry. It was they who built this shrine to the god who protects them when they are at sea.
🏠 M7 ✉ 1-1 Tsukuda, Chuo-ku 🕓 Sunrise–sunset
🚇 Tsukishima 🎫 Free

TOGO SHRINE
Set amid gardens and overlooking a lake, the shrine is a tribute to Japan's naval hero, Admiral Togo. Naïve paintings and old photographs, some hand-colored, depict his victories, notably the 1905 destruction of the Russian fleet at Tsushima.
🏠 E6 ✉ Off Meiji-dori, Harajuku, Shibuya-ku ☎ 3403–3591
🕓 Sunrise–sunset 🚇 Meijijingu-mae 🎫 Free

TOSHOGU SHRINE
This shrine, dating from 1651, is dedicated to the first Tokugawa *shogun*, Ieyasu, who died in 1616 and was quickly proclaimed divine. One of few vestiges of the early Edo period, it somehow escaped destruction in the 1868 battle between adherents of the emperor and those of the Tokugawas, when most buildings on Ueno hill were burned down. The path from the *torii* is lined by over 200 stone and bronze lanterns.
🏠 L2 ✉ 9-88 Ueno Koen, Taito-ku ☎ 3822–3455 🕓 9:30–4:30
🍴 Stalls nearby 🚇 Ueno 🎫 Moderate. Peony garden: expensive

YUSHIMA SEIDO
This shrine was founded in the 17th century for the study of Confucianism, not strictly a religion, more a philosophy and code of conduct. The shrine building is unusually austere for Japan. The first training institute for teachers was set up here in 1872, and in due course it evolved into Tokyo University.
🏠 K3 ✉ 1-4-25 Yushima, Bunkyo-ku ☎ 3251–4606
🕓 9:30–4 🚇 Ochanomizu 🎫 Free

Bronze lanterns line the path to Toshogu Shrine

Shrine etiquette
● Dress respectably.
● Pass under the *torii* (gate).
● Wash your hands thoroughly in the stone basin.
● With the dipper, pour water into your cupped hand and rinse your mouth.
● Approach the shrine and throw some coins into the slatted offertory box.
● Bow deeply twice.
● Clap your hands twice (or pull the bell rope).
● Bow once more.
(Tourists are exempt from all but the first rule.)

PARKS & GARDENS

The scenic Rikugien Garden

Landscape in miniature

The Korakuen garden was laid out in the 17th century by a refugee from Ming Dynasty China who included tiny replicas of famous Chinese lakes, rivers, and mountains. The miniature landscape even extends to growing a small field of rice, duly harvested in October. The collection of bridges ranges from simple stepping stones to the Full Moon Bridge, a half circle of stone which, with its reflection, forms a perfect 0. A huge weeping cherry tree near the gate, close to dying some years ago and unable to blossom, was saved by the botanical version of a heart transplant: new roots were grafted on to it.

See Top 25 Sights for
HAMA RIKYU GARDEN (▶ 43)
HIBIYA PARK (▶ 40)
IMPERIAL PALACE EAST GARDEN (▶ 36)
INNER GARDEN, MEIJI SHRINE (▶ 30)
SHINJUKU NATIONAL GARDEN (▶ 28)

DENBO-IN TEMPLE GARDEN

Entry to the lovely private garden of the temple is by ticket only (collect from the office next to the Asakusa pagoda, ▶ 49). The garden is reached by the temple's side gate (facing Denboin-dori, opposite Asakusa Public Hall). It was designed in the early 17th century by the tea ceremony master, Enshu Kobori. The garden pond, with resident carp and turtles, beautifully reflects the abbot's quarters and more distant pagoda.

✚ N2 ✉ Asakusa, Taito-ku 🕐 Mon–Fri 10–2:30. Closed Sat–Sun 🍴 Plenty nearby 🚇 Asakusa 💰 Free

KIYOSUMI GARDEN

Across the Sumida River opposite the Tokyo City Air Terminal, this is an oddity. A pond stocked with 10,000 carp is surrounded by many and varied rocks brought from all over Japan.

✚ N5/6 ✉ Kiyosumi, Sumida-ku ☎ 3641–5892 🕐 Daily 9–4:30 🚇 Morishita 💰 Moderate

KOISHIKAWA KORAKUEN GARDEN

Tokyo's oldest garden was laid out in the 17th century for one of the Tokugawa family, relatives of the *shogun*. Over the years, it was reduced to a quarter of the original size, and all the buildings—teahouses, gates, and shrines—were destroyed in World War II. Now

restored, it's a sanctuary for office workers with their lunch boxes, and housewives seeking some space.
📍 J3 ✉ Koraku, Bunkyo-ku ☎ 3811–3015 🕙 Tue–Sun 9–4. Closed Mon (or Tue if Mon is a national holiday), and Dec 29–Jan 3 🍴 Plenty nearby 🚇 Suidobashi 💴 Moderate

NEW OTANI HOTEL GARDEN

Next to the giant hotel is a fine traditional Japanese garden with streams and lily ponds, decorative bridges, and manicured shrubs. It continues the tradition of an early Edo-period garden on this site.
📍 G5 ✉ 4-1 Kioi-cho, Chiyoda-ku ☎ 3265–1111 🕙 Daily 9–9 🍴 In hotel 🚇 Yotsuya 💴 Moderate (free for hotel guests)

RIKUGIEN GARDEN

Widely regarded as the city's most beautiful Japanese garden, Rikugien was laid out in 1695 for a patron with literary tastes: the name means "six poem garden" and each of its scenic features was inspired by a poetic reference. Cloistered away from the noise of the city by a high brick wall, this is landscaped art of a high order, entirely artificial yet seeming natural.
📍 Off map to north ✉ 6-16-3 Honkomagomae, Bunkyo-ku ☎ 3491–2222 🕙 Tue–Sun 9–5. Closed Mon, and Dec 29–Jan 3 🚇 Sengoku, Sugamo (Toei Mita Line) 💴 Moderate

UENO PARK

The park is the home of several museums, theaters, and the zoo. Some of Tokyo's homeless sleep rough here, even in the coldest weather, and warm themselves in the sun by day. Children feed the flocks of pigeons (don't stand under the trees) and the ducks and geese on the ponds, where species from the Arctic and Siberia spend the winter.
📍 L1/2 ✉ Ueno Koen, Taito-ku 🕙 Tue–Sun sunrise–sunset. Closed Mon (Tue if Mon is a national holiday) 🍴 Restaurants and food stalls 🚇 Ueno 🚇 Ueno (Park exit). More convenient than subway 💴 Free (Museums, shrines, and the zoo charge entry fees)

YOYOGI PARK

Used by the US occupation forces after World War II, Yoyogi became the site of the Olympic Games village in 1964. The National Sports Center was built for the Games too: its stadium's pillarless roof is still strikingly modern. The park's paths, lawns, and wooded areas make a pleasant place for a stroll. For years, rock bands and other performers and their fans have gathered every Sunday afternoon along the road on the southern edge of the park.
📍 D6 ✉ Yoyogi, Shibuya-ku 🕙 5AM–5PM 🍴 Snacks 🚇 Meijijingu-mae 💴 Free

Japanese gardens

Japanese gardens generally come in three types, although larger gardens can contain the elements of more than one. **Hill gardens**, with miniature hills and a pond or stream, an island, bridges, and a meandering path, imitate nature and may allude to famous beauty spots without actually mimicking them. **Flat gardens** have few plants: rocks, raked gravel, and sand are designed to aid contemplation. **Tea gardens**, next to a teahouse, have flowing lines to contrast with the teahouse's austere simplicity.

The boating lake in Ueno Park

FOR HIGH-TECH ENTHUSIASTS

Inside Toyota's Amlux building

Market leader

For the last 30 years, Japan has been first in the field of consumer electronics, almost monopolizing every new invention—color TV, calculators, VCRs, microwave ovens, mobile phones, personal computers—for a few years while high profits can be made. Then, as the rest of the world catches up and prices fall, lower-cost manufacturers in Korea, Taiwan and China, Malaysia, and the other Asian countries take over, and Japan moves on to the next miracle product.

See Top 25 Sights for
METROPOLITAN GOVERNMENT OFFICES (► 26)
SONY CENTER (► 42)

FUJITA VENTÉ

The latest electronic and video games, including virtual reality, can be tried out here. The building is also a venue for art and architecture exhibitions.

➕ D5 ✉ Fujita Building BF, 1F, and 2F, 4-6-15 Sendagaya, Shibuya-ku ☎ 3796–2486 🕐 Fri–Wed 10–6. Closed Thu, and Dec 26–Jan 3 🍴 Snacks 🚉 Yoyogi (JR) 💷 Free (except special exhibitions)

NEC SHOWROOM

This is a hands-on exhibition of current model computers and communications technology.

➕ J6 ✉ C Plaza, Hibiya Kokusai Building B1F, Hibiya City, 2-2-3 Uchisaiwaicho, Chiyoda-ku ☎ 3595–0511 🕐 Mon–Fri 10–6. Closed Sat, Sun, and national holidays 🚉 Uchisaiwaicho 💷 Free

NTT INTERCOMMUNICATION CENTER

Science and art converge in this exhibition and interactive display of computer graphics. The "cave" filled with modifiable 3D imagery is most spectacular.

➕ C4 ✉ Tokyo Opera City Tower 4F, 3-20-2 Nishi-Shinjuku, Shinjuku-ku ☎ 0120–144199 (toll-free) 🕐 Tue–Thu, Sat–Sun 10–6; Fri 10–9. Closed Mon (Tue if Mon is a national holiday), and Dec 28–Jan 4 🍴 Restaurants 53F, 54F 🚉 Shinjuku 💷 Moderate

PENTAX GALLERY

One of the major names in photographic equipment displays a camera collection from the oldest to the newest, including novelty and disguised cameras.

➕ F8 ✉ Asahi Kogaku Building, 3-21-20 Nishi-Azabu, Minato-ku ☎ 3401–2186 🕐 Mon–Sat 10–5. Closed Sun and holidays 🍴 Nearby 🚉 Roppongi 💷 Free

TOYOTA AUTO SALON AMLUX

In a futuristic blue steel and glass tower, glossy hostesses show off even glossier cars. You can climb into every current model produced by Toyota—70 in all—and learn about the latest technical wizardry.

➕ Off map ✉ 3-3-5 Higashi-Ikebukuro, Toshima-ku ☎ 5391–5900 🕐 Tue–Sat 11–8; Sun, national holidays 10–7:30. Closed Mon (Tue if Mon is a national holiday) 🍴 Restaurant and snack bar 🚉 Higashi-Ikebukuro or Ikebukuro (7 minutes' walk) 💷 Free

YURIKAMOME WATERFRONT TRANSIT

An overhead, driverless train serves the fast-growing Tokyo Bay development of former docks, islands, and reclaimed land. It runs from Shinbashi ➕ K7 to Ariaka ➕ M10 and back; stops include the Museum of Maritime Science (► 54) and Joypolis Sega (► 62).

➕ K7–M10 ✉ Shinbashi JR Station 🕐 6AM–midnight 🚉 Shinbashi 💷 Moderate

FREE SIGHTS

Model menus

Japan's famous food replicas are much appreciated by every visitor who can't speak Japanese or read a menu. The models, *sampuru*, were first devised in the 19th century to show what new foods introduced from abroad looked like, and before plastic they were made of painted plaster and gelatine. Storekeepers were surprised when foreigners wanted to buy them, but soon adapted to the market opportunity—several shops (including Kappabashi—see main text) now sell them. Realistic replicas are not cheap—a plate of plastic noodles can cost a lot more than the real thing.

BEER MUSEUM

This is part of Yebisu Garden Place (➤ 32), reached by moving walkways from Ebisu JR Station. The Sapporo brewery here closed down; the only brewing now is in "virtual reality" headsets. Its collection of advertising posters includes a gauze-clad beauty of 1908, showing that sex as an aid to sales is no new idea.

➕ E10 ✉ 4-20-1 Ebisu, Shibuya-ku ☎ 5423–7255 🕐 Tue–Sun 10–6. Closed Mon, and Dec 28–Jan 4 🍴 Huge beer hall, restaurants, and fast-food outlets 🚇 Ebisu 🎟 Free

Advertising posters in the Beer Museum

KAPPABASHI

What Tsukiji is to fish, Kappabashi is to plates, pans, chopsticks, knives, lanterns, signs, and everything else the massive restaurant business might need (except food—the stores here sell only the plastic variety). A huge head crowned with a chef's hat stands on top of a tall building to mark the beginning of Kappabashi-dori, where most of the stores are.

➕ M2 ✉ Kappabashi-dori, Taito-ku 🕐 Shops: Mon–Sat 9:30–6:30 approx. 🍴 Wide choice 🚇 Tawaramachi 🎟 Free

ORIGAMI KAIKAN

You can watch work going on in the factory and demonstrations of *origami*, the art of paper folding. Special papers and paper crafts are sold in the shop.

➕ K3 ✉ 1-7-14 Yushima, Bunkyo-ku ☎ 3811–4025 🕐 Mon–Sat 9–5. Closed Sun and national holidays 🍴 Snacks nearby 🚇 Ochanomizu JR and subway (5 minutes' walk) 🎟 Free

PHILATELIC MUSEUM

Superb collections of Japanese and other stamps, as well as postal history exhibits, are on display.

➕ D5 ✉ Yushu Kaikan Building 4F, 2-2-10 Yoyogi, Shibuya-ku ☎ 3379–1433 🕐 Tue, Thu, Sat 1–5. Closed national holidays and early August 🍴 Plenty nearby 🚇 Shinjuku 🎟 Free

SUMO MUSEUM

A store of records, relics, and pictures of past *yokozuna*—the grand masters of *sumo* wrestling—is housed in the building that is also the main arena for matches. You may see some of today's stars arriving.

➕ N4 ✉ 1-3-28 Yokoami, Sumida-ku ☎ 3622–0366 🕐 9:30–4:30. Closed during tournaments, except to ticket-holders 🍴 Snacks 🚇 Ryogoku (JR) 🎟 Free

ATTRACTIONS FOR CHILDREN

See Top 25 Sights for
SHITAMACHI MUSEUM (➤ 48)
SONY CENTER (➤ 42)
TOKYO DISNEYLAND (➤ 50)

Toshima-en

This elaborate amusement park, set in a northwestern suburb, has some of the wildest rollercoaster rides, loops, corkscrews, and spins to be found anywhere, including a "zero-gravity" long, free fall. There are also plenty of gentler rides to suit smaller children, as well as a waterpark with several pools and slides.

🚇 Off map ✉ 3-25-1 Koyama, Nerima-ku 3990–3131 🕐 10–5. Closed Tue 🍴 Snacks and fast food 🚉 Toshima-en (Seibu-Ikebukuro Line) 💰 Expensive

HANAYASHIKI

An amusement park founded in 1853. The mainly traditional rides include carousels, bumper cars, and a haunted house, all aimed at younger children.

🚇 N2 ✉ 2-28-1 Asakusa, Taito-ku ☎ 3842–8780 🕐 Wed–Mon 10–6. Closed Tue except in school holidays 🍴 Snacks 🚉 Asakusa 💰 Expensive

JOYPOLIS SEGA

A virtual reality theme park with thrilling "rides" and many video games. Next to the Odaiba beach area.

🚇 Off map ✉ 1-6-1 Daiba, Minato-ku ☎ 5500–1801 🕐 Daily 10AM–11:30PM 🍴 Café and restaurant 🚉 Odaiba Kaihinkoen (Yurikamome Waterfront Transit from Shinbushi, ➤ 60) 💰 Moderate

KORAKUEN

This fairground and amusement park features a giant roller-coaster, the "Ultra Twister", and loop-the-loop train, as well as gentler rides for younger children. The entry ticket does not include the cost of rides.

🚇 J3 ✉ 1-3-61 Koraku, Bunkyo-ku ☎ 5800–9999 🕐 Daily 10–6 🍴 Snack bars and food stalls 🚉 Korakuen, Suidobashi 🚉 Suidobashi 💰 Expensive

NATIONAL CHILDREN'S CASTLE

A complete entertainment center with a swimming pool, concert hall, cinema, and theater. There's a program of special classes in dance, music, and crafts.

🚇 E7 ✉ 5-53-1 Jingumae, Shibuya-ku ☎ 3797–5666 🕐 Tue–Fri 12:30–5:30; Sat, Sun, holidays 10:30–5:30. Closed Mon 🍴 Restaurant and snacks 🚉 Omotesando 💰 Moderate

NHK BROADCASTING CENTER

Just south of Yoyogi Park, the NHK runs tours of the sets used for their TV programs. Performances are in Japanese.

🚇 D7 ✉ 2-2-1 Jinnan, Shibuya-ku ☎ 3485–8034 🕐 Tue–Sun 10–6. Closed Mon (Tue if Mon is a national holiday) 🍴 Snacks 🚉 Meijijingu-mae, Shibuya 💰 Moderate

SHINAGAWA AQUARIUM (SUIZOKUKAN)

A well-stocked aquarium with a walk-through glass tunnel, so you can feel surrounded by sharks. Performing sealions and dolphins give regular shows.

🚇 Off map ✉ 3-2-1 Katsushima, Shinagawa-ku ☎ 3762–3431 🕐 Wed–Mon 10–5. Closed Tue, and Dec 29–Jan 1 🍴 Snacks 🚉 Omorikaigan (Keihin-Kyuko Line from Shinagawa) 💰 Moderate

Young visitors can view the underwater acrobatics of Shinagawa Aquarium's sea-life from a glass tunnel

TOKYO
where to...

JAPANESE RESTAURANTS

Prices

The price guides given for Japanese restaurants (► 64–66) are for set menus, known as "sets;" most restaurants offer a choice of these. Lunch sets cost much less than dinner.

$ = up to ¥3,000
$$ = ¥3,000–¥6,000
$$$ = over ¥6,000

Choices

Bento: boxed lunch.

Kaiseki ryori: refined cuisine of many small delicacies, using typically Japanese ingredients.

Kushiage: deep-fried morsels on sticks.

Ramen: Chinese noodles, in soups, usually with pork.

Robatayaki: cooking over charcoal grill.

Shabu-shabu: thin slices of beef swirled in a boiling broth, then dipped in sauces.

Soba: buckwheat-flour noodles.

Sukiyaki: thinly sliced beef cooked at the table with vegetables and *tofu*.

Teishoku: set meal/fixed-price menu.

Tempura: shrimp, fish, and vegetables coated in a light batter and deep fried.

Teppanyaki: fish, meat, and vegetables cooked on a griddle.

Udon: wheat-flour noodles.

Yakitori: small pieces of chicken, liver, or other meat, grilled on bamboo skewers.

FUROSATO ($$)

Traditional country food in a picturesque old mountain farmhouse reconstructed here. Fish, chicken, and vegetables grilled over a *hibachi* (small charcoal grill) are a specialty.

➕ D9 ✉ 3-4-1 Aobadai, Meguro-ku ☎ 3463–2310
🕐 Daily 5–11
Ⓜ Nakameguro, Shibuya

FUTABA ($)

Ueno is known especially for *tonkatsu*, fried pork cutlet, eaten with rice, soup, and pickled vegetables, and this is one of the oldest restaurants serving it.

➕ L2 ✉ 2-8-11 Ueno, Taito-ku ☎ 3831–6483
🕐 Daily 11:30–2:30, 5–7:30
Ⓜ Ueno

HAN ($$)

One of a chain, with real Japanese atmosphere and traditional home cooking, busy with groups of businessmen, young couples, maybe a gang of girls eating at the counter. A keen young man kneels to take your order, tapping it into his hand-held terminal. Lots of small dishes give you a chance to try new experiences or old favorites.

➕ H7 ✉ 4-3-20 Toranomon, Minato-ku ☎ 3578–8293
🕐 Daily 11:30–2, 5–11
Ⓜ Kamiyacho

HASSAN ($$)

A busy traditional restaurant with a choice of *tatami* (straw mats) or chairs. The set menus of *tempura*, *sukiyaki*, and *shabu-shabu* include all-you-can-eat options, at a higher price, for the very hungry.

➕ G8 ✉ 6-1-20 Roppongi B1F, Minato-ku ☎ 3403–8333
🕐 Daily 11:30–2, 5–11
Ⓜ Roppongi

HIGO BATTEN ($$)

Tasty combinations of fish and shellfish, vegetables, and meats grilled on bamboo skewers. Traditional décor of black wood and white screens.

➕ F7 ✉ AG Building 1F, 3-18-17 Minami-Aoyama, Minato-ku ☎ 3423–4462
🕐 Daily 5–11:15
Ⓜ Omotesando

JINYA ($$)

Family-style Japanese cooking, beautifully presented. Seating on *tatami* mats or at conventional tables.

➕ D4 ✉ My City Building 7F, Shinjuku Station, 3-38-1 Shinjuku-ku ☎ 3352–0018
🕐 Daily 4–midnight
Ⓜ Shinjuku

KISOJI ($)

A convenient Ginza spot for budget, set-menu lunches of soup and rice with fish or chicken.

➕ K6 ✉ Ginza Jujiya Building 5F, 3-5-4 Ginza, Chuo-ku ☎ 3567–0406 🕐 Daily 11:30–2:30, 5–9 Ⓜ Ginza

KONOMI ($$$)

A small restaurant in the Kappabashi district, specializing in the cuisine of Kyoto. *Kyobento*, a double-decker lacquer-box lunch of two dozen beautiful little seasonal dishes, is an aesthetic treat.

➕ M2 ✉ 1-7-2 Nishi-Asakusa, Taito-ku ☎ 3843–7773
🕐 Mon–Fri 12–3, 5–10; Sat–Sun 5–10 Ⓜ Tawaramachi

NAKASE ($$$)

A famous and long-established *tempura* restaurant near Nakamise-dori. Follow your nose to the delicious smells, but be prepared to wait. Often the line forms outside the door well before opening time. Lunch is the best—for economy and because the area shuts early.

✚ N2 ✉ 1-39-13 Asakusa, Taito-ku ☎ 3841–4015
🕒 Wed–Mon noon–8. Closed Tue Ⓢ Asakusa

ROPPONGI SUMIDA ($$$)

Teppanyaki grilled delicacies expertly prepared from fresh crab, abalone, shrimp, and other seafoods, and steak.

✚ G7 ✉ Aoda Roppongi Building B1F, 3-16-33 Roppongi, Minato-ku ☎ 5570–5777
🕒 Mon–Fri 11:30–2:30, 5:30–10. Closed Sat, Sun, and holidays Ⓢ Roppongi

SAKAFUJI ($)

A bright and friendly modern restaurant on three floors, next to Hotel TOP. *Yakitori, kushiage, tempura,* and *teppanyaki* are among the many choices.

✚ M2 ✉ 1-6-1 Asakusa, Taito-ku ☎ 3843–1122
🕒 Tue–Sun 11–10.30. Closed Mon Ⓢ Asakusa

SERETA ($$)

Run by the charming Sera family, specializing in *yakitori*. Sit at the counter, and sizzling skewers of pork, chicken livers, and other morsels will appear in rapid succession.

✚ G7 ✉ 6-2-31, B1F, Roppongi Minato-ku (under Nissan showroom)
☎ 3405–2882 🕒 Daily

11:30–2, 5:30–11
Ⓢ Roppongi

SHABU ZEN ($$)

A big restaurant specializing in *shabu-shabu*, and including all-you-can-eat deals. The American beef is less costly than the local.

✚ G8 ✉ 5-17-16 Roppongi, Minato-ku ☎ 3585–5388
🕒 Daily 5–11:30 Ⓢ Roppongi
Also at:
✚ K7 ✉ Gonza Core Building, 5-8-20 Ginza, Chou-ku
Ⓢ Higashi-Ginza

SHIGEYOSHI ($$$)

A small counter and a few tables, with the chefs in full view. The cooking is traditional, from the Nagoya area. Lunch prices are reasonable.

✚ E7 ✉ Olympia Co-op B1F, 6-35-3 Jingumae, Shibuya-ku ☎ 3400–4044 🕒 Mon–Fri 11:30–2, 5:30–10:30; Sat–Sun 5:30–10:30 Ⓢ Meijijingu-mae

TSUKIJI ($$)

A bright and busy all-day restaurant in the heart of Ginza. Often crowded. The set menus at lunchtime are attractive and reasonably priced.

✚ K7 ✉ Miyuki Building B1F, 5-6-12 Ginza, Chuo-ku ☎ 3571–0071 🕒 Daily 8:30–7 Ⓢ Higashi-Ginza

TSUNAHACHI ($)

Noted especially for fine quality *tempura* at a surprisingly fair price, particularly if you stick to the set menus.

✚ D4 ✉ 3-31-8 Shinjuku, Shinjuku-ku ☎ 3352–1011 🕒 Daily 11–2, 5–9 Ⓢ Shinjuku San-chome

Etiquette

● After wiping your fingers on the moist towel (*oshibori*) brought before your meal, roll it up and keep it for use as a napkin.

● Drink soup from the bowl as if it were a cup. Pick out solid pieces with chopsticks. Slurping soup and noodles is approved.

● Rice is usually eaten by holding the bowl close to your mouth and using chopsticks.

● Don't point with chopsticks, or lick the ends, or put the ends that go in your mouth into a communal dish. Don't leave chopsticks crossed.

● If you can't manage something with chopsticks, ask for a knife (*naifu*), fork (*foku*), and spoon (*supun*).

● Never blow your nose in a restaurant. Find somewhere to hide first.

● Pour drinks for your companions; leave it to them to pour yours. When they do, it's polite to hold your glass up to be filled.

SUSHI & SASHIMI

What is *sushi*?

Among Westerners, plenty of fallacies exist on the subject of *sushi* and *sashimi*. "It's raw fish, right?" Not exactly. Morsels of raw fish, shellfish, and roes, as well as a few cooked varieties, pressed on to a pad of warm, vinegared rice—that's *sushi* (or more precisely, *nigirizushi*). Pieces of fish and vegetable rolled in rice and seaweed are *makizushi*. Delicate slices of raw fish and shellfish served with *daikon* (shredded white radish), *wasabi* (green horseradish paste), and soy sauce—that's *sashimi*, often served as a first course. If prices are not posted, ask—or you may face a shock along with the check.

EDO-GIN ($$)

Well-established and popular, serving *sashimi* and *sushi* made from the freshest fish from the nearby market. You can see some of it still swimming in a tank.

✚ K7 ✉ 4-5-1 Tsukiji, Chuo-ku ☎ 3543–4401 🕐 Daily 10–10. Closed Sun, every second Mon, and some national holidays 🚇 Tsukiji

GENROKUZUSHI ($)

An economical way to eat *sushi*: little dishes, each containing two pieces, circle past you on a conveyor belt and you pick those that take your fancy. The chefs work to replace the *sushi* while they chat to the customers.

✚ E7 ✉ 5-8-5 Jingumae, Shibuya-ku ☎ 3498–3968 🕐 Daily 11–9 🚇 Meijijingu-mae

Also at:

✚ N2 ✉ 1-2-3 Hanakawado, Taito-ku 🚇 Asakusa

KAITEN-ZUSHI ($)

Another rotating counter that carries the choices slowly past you. It's basic good-quality *sushi*, charged per piece (always a pair) at budget prices, in the heart of Ginza.

✚ K6 ✉ Kyodo Building B1F, 2-8-15 Ginza, Chuo-ku ☎ 3564–2453 🕐 Daily 10:30–9:30 🚇 Ginza

KYUBEI ($$$)

Founded many years ago, and still going strong, with some of the most expertly made *sushi* to be found anywhere.

✚ K7 ✉ 8-7-6 Ginza, Chuo-ku ☎ 3572–3704 🕐 Mon–Sat 11:30–2, 5–10. Closed Sun 🚇 Higashi-Ginza

RYU SUSHI ($$)

It is hard to get any nearer to the source of supply than this little *sushi* bar next to the market halls. Unusually for the Tsukiji location, the owner is not the senior chef but another sort of artist, the painter Ryutaro Shiina. He is often in attendance from an early hour, greeting the customers, who mostly work in the market. It's a great place to satisfy your hunger after a pre-dawn visit there.

✚ K7 ✉ 5-2-1 Tsukiji, Chuo-ku ☎ 3541–9517 🕐 Market days only 7AM–2PM. Closed Sun, national holidays, and market holidays 🚇 Tsukiji

TAKENO ($$$)

Fine quality *sashimi* and *sushi* fresh from the market. Most of the lunchtime customers are market professionals; the evening crowd comes from far and wide. At the *sushi* counter, the chefs keep their jewel-like creations coming until you reluctantly call a halt.

✚ K7 ✉ 6-21-2 Tsukiji, Chuo-ku ☎ 3541–8698 🕐 Mon–Sat 11–9. Closed Sun and holidays 🚇 Tsukiji

TAMAZUSHI ($)

Quick service of good *sushi*, with economical set menus and *à la carte*, depending on what is in season. At lunchtime, you may have to wait for the business crowd to clear.

✚ K7 ✉ B2F Ginza Core Building, 5-8-20 Ginza, Chuo-ku ☎ 3573–0057 🕐 Mon–Sat 11–10; Sun, holidays 12–9 🚇 Higashi-Ginza

ITALIAN RESTAURANTS

CAPRICCIOSA ($)
Cheerful décor, and large portions of pasta and other Mediterranean standards at a fair price. One of a chain with branches in several areas.
G7 7-13-2 Roppongi, Minato-ku 5410–6061
Daily 11–11 Roppongi

IL BOCCALONE ($$$)
With the look and atmosphere of a *trattoria* in northern Italy, serving good *antipasti*, grills, risotto, and notable desserts.
E9 1-15-9 Ebisu, Shibuya-ku 3449–1430
Daily 11:30–2:30, 5–11 Ebisu

LA BOHÈME ($$)
Various pastas and sauces, pizzas, salads, and ice creams. Popular with night owls.
E7 Jubilee Plaza B1F, 5-8-5 Jingumae, Shibuya-ku 5467–5888 Daily 11:30AM–4AM Omotesando

LA GRANATA ($$)
An informal *trattoria* serving authentic Italian food, made with fine fresh ingredients.
G6 TBS Kaikan Building B1F, 5-3-3 Akasaka, Minato-ku 3582–5891 Daily 11–10 Akasaka

LA VERDE ($)
Noted for large servings of pasta with tasty toppings, at budget prices.
F6 Aoyama Building B1F, Kita-Aoyama, Minato-ku 3404–0712 Daily 11:30–2:30, 5:30–11 Aoyama-itchome
Also at:
E7 1-7-2 Jingumae, Shinbuya-ku Harajuku (JR)

LA VERDE TRATTORIA ($$)
An unpretentious and friendly restaurant serving tasty *antipasti*, a huge choice of pastas, 21 pizzas (including some unusual toppings), and fresh homemade desserts.
J7 Fukoku Seimei Building B1F, 2-2-2 Uchisaiwaicho, Chiyoda-ku 3591–4030 Daily 11:30–10 Uchisaiwaicho

PENDIO ROSSO ($$)
Fresh, colorful salads, seafood, and steaks, in a Japanese version of Mediterranean cooking. In the same building as the Suntory Museum (➤ 53).
G6 1-2-3 Moto-Akasaka 1F, Minato-ku 3470–1101
Daily 11:30–2, 5–11 Akasakamitsuke

ROSSI ($$)
An appetizing and varied menu of mainly Tuscan food: veal, lamb, and *osso buco* are specialties. Pasta set menus are available at lunchtime.
G7 7-17-12 Roppongi, Minato-ku 3405–1232
Mon–Sat 11:30–2, 6–11:30. Closed Sun and holidays
Roppongi

ROSSO E NERO ($$)
Home cooking, with good *antipasti*, a wide choice of pastas and sauces, and grills. Reflecting the chef's background, the menu includes Austrian as well as Italian dishes, notably the fruit *strudel* and dumpling desserts.
G5 Kioi-cho Building 2F, 3-12 Kioi-cho, Chiyoda-ku 3237–5888 Daily 11:30–2, 5:30–11 Nagatacho

Prices

The price guides given for non-Japanese restaurants (➤ 67–71) are for an average meal (starter and main course, or main course and dessert) per head, including service but excluding drinks.

$ = up to ¥3,000
$$ = ¥3,000–¥6,000
$$$ = over ¥6,000

Lintaro ($$)

Lintaro Mizuhama is the friendly owner of the restaurant that bears his name, and he is often to be found chatting to the diners or directing the service. He's a Ginza native and expert: his family has been here for centuries. The deep basement room is a surprise, with its high ceiling and Renaissance pictures. The food is Italian but with an added Japanese flair in its presentation and some of the flavors. Superbly fresh salads and vegetables come from the restaurant's special gardens.
K7 5-9-15 Ginza, Chuo-ku 3571–2037
Daily 11–2:30, 5–11. Closed New Year holiday
Ginza

INDIAN & SRI LANKAN RESTAURANTS

AJANTA ($)
An old favorite, with the simplest of settings but one of the most comprehensive menus in Tokyo. The dishes are as authentic as you will find.
✚ G5 ✉ 3-11 Nibancho, Chiyoda-ku ☎ 3264–6955 🕐 Daily 24 hours 🚇 Kojimachi

ASHOKA ($$)
In a rather luxurious setting overlooking Chuo-dori, Ginza's high street, and serving a wide range of traditional dishes, curries, and tasty *tandoori*-cooked chicken. Freshly made yogurt desserts are a specialty.
✚ K7 ✉ Pearl Building 2F, 7-9-18 Ginza, Chuo-ku ☎ 3572–2377 🕐 Mon–Sat 11:30–9:30; Sun 12–8:30 🚇 Higashi-Ginza

CEYLON INN ($)
The tables occupy several connecting rooms in an old house, with folk-art decoration contributing to the Sri Lankan atmosphere. Serves colorful curries and *sambals*, cooling salads, and fruits.
✚ D10 ✉ 2-7-8 Kami-Meguro, Meguro-ku ☎ 3716–0440 🕐 Daily 11–2:30, 5–11 🚇 Nakameguro

KENBOKKE ($)
The décor here is modern with few Indian touches, but the Bombay-born chef produces authentic dishes. The *tandoori* shrimp and chicken are specialties.
✚ F8 ✉ Empire Building 2F, 4-1-28 Nishi-Azabu, Minato-ku ☎ 3498–7080 🕐 Daily 11:30–11 🚇 Hiroo

Tomoca ($$)
This is an agreeable, relaxed Sri Lankan restaurant where you select your curry, choosing from shrimp, fish, chicken, or beef, and specify the degree of spiciness. (Don't ask for the hottest unless your digestive tract is made from Teflon.) A whole range of extras comes with it: poppadums, salads, fried eggplant, *dal*, and tangy *sambals*.
✚ E4 ✉ 1-7-27 Yotsuya, Shinjuku-ku ☎ 3353–7945 🕐 Daily 11–10:30 🚇 Shinjukugyoen-mae

MOTI ($)
One of five branches (others include Roppongi) of an old favorite of locals and expatriates alike. Standard Indian décor and menu, with tasty vegetarian dishes, *kormas* and chicken *masala*.
✚ H7 ✉ Kinpa Building 3F, 2-14-31 Akasaka, Minato-ku ☎ 3584–6640 🕐 Mon–Sat 11:30–11; Sun 12–10 🚇 Akasaka

MUGHAL ($)
In a cozy basement, serving good shrimp, chicken and mutton curries, *tandoori* dishes, and crisp salads.
✚ H6 ✉ Commerce Building B1F, 3-10-2 Akasaka, Minato-ku ☎ 3582–9940 🕐 Daily 11:30–10:30 🚇 Akasaka-mitsuke

PALETTE ($)
A plain and simple café where Sri Lankan chefs will make the curries as hot as you choose, or as mild. The breads and desserts are excellent.
✚ E9 ✉ 1-16-8 Nishi-Ebisu, Shibuya-ku ☎ 5489–0770 🕐 Daily 11:30–10:30 🚇 Ebisu

SAMRAT ($)
One of the first of the Indian wave and still popular, serving *tandoori* dishes and curries on the milder side. The buffet represents good value for money.
✚ G7 ✉ Shojikiya Building 3F, 4-10-10 Roppongi, Minato-ku ☎ 3496–9410 🕐 Daily 5–10 🚇 Roppongi
Also at:
✚ D8 ✉ Koyasu One Building 6F, 13-7 Udagawacho, Shibuya-ku 🚇 Shibuya

THAI RESTAURANTS

BENJARONG ($$)

An elegant restaurant, and cuisine to match, beautifully prepared by the former chef of a top Bangkok hotel. The menu is fully explained in English. Lunch prices are much lower than dinner.
✚ D4 ☒ Miyata Building 2F, 1-4-12 Kabukicho, Shinjuku-ku ☎ 3209–7064 ◷ Mon–Sat 11:30–2, 5:30–10:30. Closed Sun ☻ Shinjuku

CHIANG MAI ($$)

Customers are crammed into two small rooms to savor the standard dishes, cooked by two Thai chefs. Try the *tom yam gung* soup, the tangy fresh salads, and the spicy chicken.
✚ K6 ☒ 1-6-10 Yurakucho, Chiyoda-ku ☎ 3580–0456 ◷ Daily 11–11 ☻ Hibiya

EREWAN ($$)

An elegant restaurant with a fine view. A full range of authentic Thai cooking is served, delicate or fiery according to your taste. Popular with an expat and diplomatic crowd.
✚ G8 ☒ Roi Building 13F, 5-5-1 Roppongi, Minato-ku ☎ 3404–5741 ◷ Daily 11:30–2, 5:30–11 ☻ Roppongi

KAEWJAI ($$)

It's close to the Thai Embassy and popular with the staff there, so the food and ambience are as authentic as any in Tokyo. The lunch buffet is a relative bargain and worth the journey to Shinagawa.
✚ Off map ☒ 2-14-9 Kami Osaki, Shinagawa-ku ☎ 5420–7727 ◷ Daily 11:30–10:30 ☻ Meguro (JR Yamanote Line)

MAI-THAI ($$)

A small, cheerful and popular spot on a side street, serving a typical Thai menu at reasonable prices. One of a growing choice of eating places in the Ebisu area.
✚ E9 ☒ 1-18-16 Ebisu, Shibuya-ku ☎ 3280–1155 ◷ Daily 11:30–2:30, 5–11 ☻ Ebisu

RICE TERRACE ($$)

A relaxed setting for enjoying some of the best Thai food in Tokyo. The service is friendly but polished. Try to get a table downstairs: the upper level is cramped.
✚ F8 ☒ 2-7-9 Nishi-Azabu, Minato-ku ☎ 3498–6271 ◷ Daily 11:30–2, 5:30–11 ☻ Nogizaka

SIAM ($$)

A cut above the rest in this entertainment district, this restaurant specializes in northern Thai cooking. Intriguing spice combinations make the long menu, explained in English, quite an adventure.
✚ D4 ☒ Umemura Building 2F, 1-3-11 Kabukicho, Shinjuku-ku ☎ 3232–6300 ◷ Daily 5PM–3AM ☻ Shinjuku

THE SIAM ($)

This one has been around for years, and it is still serving tasty Thai standards at economical prices, for Ginza, especially at lunchtime.
✚ K7 ☒ World Town Building 8F, 5-8-17 Ginza, Chuo-ku ☎ 3572–4101 ◷ Daily 11:30–2, 5:30–11 ☻ Higashi-Ginza

Gold Leaf ($$$)

In Tokyo as in most of the world, it seems, Thai food is booming. This is one of the most attractive places in Tokyo to eat it, with a décor of teak wood and black lacquer complementing the colorful dishes. Bangkok-trained chefs prepare subtly spiced salads, soups laced with the quintessential Thai ingredients of lemongrass, coriander, chilli, and coconut milk, and delicious curries. Service is polished and the menu explains it all in English.
✚ F9 ☒ Taisei Koki Building B1F, 5-4-12 Hiroo, Shibuya-ku ☎ 3447–1212 ◷ Daily 11:30–2, 5:30–10 ☻ Hiroo

OTHER INTERNATIONAL EATING

Sounds familiar

The Japanese have adapted the words as well as adopting the food:

hot dog: *hotto doggu*

hamburger: *hambaga*

sandwich: *sando-ichi*

steak: *suteki*

ham: *hamu*

sausage: *soseji*

salad: *sarada*

bread: *pan*

butter : *bata*

coffee: *kohi*

bacon and egg: *bekon eggu*

orange juice: *orenji jusu*

ice cream: *aisu kurimu*

chocolate cake: *chokoreto keiki*

ASENA ($$): TURKISH

Authentic *meze* (hors d'oeuvres) and kebabs, and much more, with a belly-dance show every Friday and Saturday.

✚ G6 ✉ 5-5-11 Akasaka, Minato-ku ☎ 3505–5282 🕐 Daily 5–11 Ⓡ Akasaka

BENGAWAN SOLO ($$): INDONESIAN

Indonesian décor, staff, and cooking. The colorful, multi-dish *rijsttafel*, including some highly spiced items, gives you a chance to experience the widest variety.

✚ G7 ✉ Kanako Building 1F, 7-18-13 Roppongi, Minato-ku ☎ 3403–3031 🕐 Mon–Sat 11:30–2:30, 5–10. Closed Sun Ⓡ Roppongi

BOUGAINVILLEA ($$): VIETNAMESE

Vietnamese food may yet challenge Thai for the "ethnic" crown. This place has a wide choice of authentic dishes: noodle soups, crab with coriander, spring rolls, sweet and sour pork or chicken, meatballs, crisp salads.

✚ D8 ✉ Romanee Building 2F, 2-25-9 Dogenzaka, Shibuya-ku ☎ 3496–5537 🕐 Daily 11:30–2, 5–11 Ⓡ Shibuya

CLUB KREISEL ($$): GERMAN

Wurst, sauerkraut, potatoes, *wienerschnitzel*, and the delicious red-fruit dessert called *rote grütze*. Beer and *sekt* at reasonable prices.

✚ G6 ✉ OAG Haus 1F, 7-5-56 Akasaka, Minato-ku ☎ 3583–9487 🕐 Daily 5–11 Ⓡ Akasaka

OH-HO ($$): CHINESE

A bright and spacious restaurant serving authentic Cantonese and Taiwanese dishes. Live music in the evenings.

✚ G7 ✉ Nittaku Building B1F, 3-8-15 Roppongi, Minato-ku ☎ 3479–2881 🕐 Mon–Sat 5PM–5AM; Sun 5PM–11PM Ⓡ Roppongi

PATIO FLAMENCO ($$$): SPANISH

Paella is the specialty. Flamenco performances, three shows nightly.

✚ D8 ✉ 2-10-12 Dogenzaka, Shibuya-ku ☎ 3496–2753 🕐 Daily 5:30–11 Ⓡ Shibuya

ROSITA ($): MEXICAN

All the expected dishes—guacamole, tacos, *enchilladas*, chili con carne—in a folksy atmosphere.

✚ D4 ✉ Pegas-Kan Building B1F, 3-31-5 Shinjuku, Shinjuku-ku ☎ 3356–7538 🕐 Mon–Sat 11:30–2:30, 5:30–11. Closed Sun Ⓡ Shinjuku San-chome

SAMOVAR ($$): RUSSIAN

Authentic Russian stews and soups, kebabs, rye bread, beers, and vodkas.

✚ D8 ✉ 2-22-5 Dogenzaka, Shibuya-ku ☎ 3462–0648 🕐 Mon–Sat 5–11. Closed Sun Ⓡ Shibuya

TOKAI-EN ($): KOREAN

An enormous operation, with all-you-can-eat bargain lunches. Spicy seafood, stews, and *bulgogi* barbecues are specialties. It can get boisterous in the late evening.

✚ D4 ✉ 1-6-3 Kabukicho, Shinjuku-ku ☎ 3200–2934 🕐 11AM–4AM Ⓡ Shinjuku

BURGERS, DINERS, & DELIS

DOLE FRUIT CAFÉ ($)
Fresh fruits and vegetables come as juices, and in tasty combinations such as curries and pizzas. Many dishes are vegetarian
✚ D8 ✉ Kokusai Building A-Kan 2F, 13–16 Udagawa-cho, Shibuya-ku ☎ 3464–6030
🕐 Daily 11–10 🚇 Shibuya

DON-DON ($)
An all-day, all-night economy diner, serving basic rice-bowl dishes—rice and beef, rice and curry—at budget prices.
✚ H6 ✉ 3-6-9 Akasaka, Minato-ku ☎ 3585–8920
🕐 Daily 24 hours 🚇 Akasaka-mitsuke

FARM GRILL ($)
A big, friendly place serving modern American salads, steaks, chili, pastas, plus *teriyaki* chicken; reasonably priced drinks.
✚ K6 ✉ Ginza Nine Sangokan Building 2F, 1-8-5 Ginza, Chuo-ku ☎ 5568–6156 🕐 Daily 11:30–2:30, 5–11 🚇 Ginza-itchome

GIRAFFE ($)
A cheerful café that concentrates on serving beer and a short menu of fast food and snacks, Japanese-style.
✚ D8 ✉ BIR Building 1F, 32-15 Udagawa-cho, Shibuya-ku ☎ 3770–5577 🕐 Daily 11–11 🚇 Shibuya

HARD ROCK CAFÉ ($$)
Hamburgers, salads and snacks, ice creams and pie, to loud music. Long lines form on weekends.
✚ G8 ✉ 5-4-20 Roppongi, Minato-ku ☎ 3408–7018
🕐 Daily 11AM–midnight
🚇 Roppongi

HOMEWORKS ($)
Above-average hamburgers with all the add-ons; plus salads, sandwiches, and snacks.
✚ F9 ✉ Shichiseisha Building 1F, 5-1-20 Hiroo, Shibuya-ku ☎ 3444–4560 🕐 Mon–Sat 11–9; Sun and holidays 11–6 🚇 Hiroo

JOHNNY ROCKETS ($)
Good hamburgers, french fries, salads, and other fast-food staples.
✚ G7 ✉ Coco Roppongi Building 2F, 3-11-10 Roppongi, Minato-ku ☎ 3423–1955
🕐 Sun–Thu 11–11; Fri–Sat 11AM–6AM 🚇 Roppongi

NEWS DELI ($)
New York deli foods—salads, soups, sandwiches, pastas, and grills. Counter and tables; takeout service.
✚ E7 ✉ SJ Building 1F, 3-6-26 Kita-Aoyama, Minato-ku ☎ 3407–1715 🕐 Daily 11–11 🚇 Omotesando

ROCK 'N' ROLL DINER ($)
American-style salads, hamburgers and sandwiches in a big, busy 60s environment.
✚ A7 ✉ Big Ben Building B1F, 2-5-2 Kitazawa, Setagaya-ku ☎ 3411–6565 🕐 Sun–Thu 5PM–midnight; Fri–Sat 4PM–2AM 🚇 Yoyogi-uehara

VICTORIA STATION ($$)
Elaborately themed as an old London train station and carriages. A lot of diners go for the salad bar and roast rib of beef.
✚ H6 ✉ 3-15-13 Akasaka, Minato-ku ☎ 3586–0711
🕐 Mon–Sat 11AM–midnight; Sun and holidays 11–10
🚇 Roppongi, Akasaka-mitsuke

Fusion food
California and Australian chefs devised "Pacific Rim" cuisine by combining Japanese with other Asian fare. A similar process in reverse has produced a crop of restaurants in Tokyo where the dishes are Western with a local twist. One such is Bistro de Maido ($$), run by Hiroyuki Masuda. His informal restaurant in a Shibuya basement is popular with young business people. Salads topped with lightly seared seafoods are a specialty.
✚ D7 ✉ Miyagi Building B1F, 1-10-12 Shibuya, Shibuya-ku ☎ 3407–5724
🕐 Daily 5:30–11:30PM. Closed Dec 31–Jan 4 🚇 Shibuya

Big chains
The big names in fast food are springing up all over the city, and not just to satisfy foreign tastes. The Japanese have an appetite for hamburgers and fried chicken, too. You'll see McDonald's, Wendy's , KFC, Burger King, and Subway, as well as many local chains and single outlets. And, of course, a lot of Japanese food lends itself to almost instant service.

SHOPPING DISTRICTS

Shopping is almost a national mania. It took only a few decades of prosperity to turn a frugal people into addicts of conspicuous consumption. Many shops open every day, typical hours being 10–6 or 10–7. There's always some sort of promotion; the marketing wizards never let up. Any excuse will do for a sales push, especially a holiday or festival. Large purchases for export will be free of sales tax (carry your passport). In shops that don't expect foreigners, prices may be written in unfamiliar characters. Just ask: *Ikura desu-ka*? ("How much?")

Price of paradise

The shops are a pleasure to visit, the range and quality of goods outstanding, the displays beautiful, the service usually impeccable. The customer is always right. Your most mundane purchase will be wrapped as though it were a jewel beyond price. Inflation has been low for decades, and with most foreign currencies increasing in value compared with the yen in recent years, prices are much more reasonable than they used to be.

AKIHABARA

For electrical and electronic equipment. At the JR station, look for signs to Electric Town, on the west side, where seven- and eight-floor buildings are stuffed with appliances piled in apparent confusion.
✚ L3 🚇 Akihabara
🚇 Akihabara (JR)

ASAKUSA

Nakamise-dori, near the temple, is a street of little traditional shops of all kinds.
✚ N2 🚇 Asakusa

GINZA-YURAKUCHO

For the famous department stores on Chuo-dori and in Yurakucho, and specialist shops, craft shops, and antique shops, from Ginza 4-chome through 7-chome.
✚ K6/7 🚇 Ginza, Yurakucho, Higashi-Ginza

JINGUMAE/HARAJUKU

Takeshita-dori for youth fashions and fads; Omotesando-dori for higher fashion and higher prices.
✚ E7 🚇 Meijijingu-mae, Omotesando

KANDA-JINBOCHO

An area with many secondhand bookstores stocking Japanese and foreign books, and woodblock prints.
✚ J4 🚇 Jinbocho

MINAMI-AOYAMA

Antique shops along and around Kotto-dori; fashion stores on Aoyama-dori and Omotesando-dori.
✚ F6/7 🚇 Omotesando

SHIBUYA

For department stores, fashion boutiques, bookstores, and home improvement stores.
✚ D8 🚇 Shibuya

SHINJUKU

Camera and audiovisual equipment stores west and east of the station; department stores above and east of the station.
✚ D/E4 🚇 Shinjuku, Shinjuku San-chome

UENO

The Ameyoko (short for Ameya Yokocho) market is packed with stalls selling groceries, household goods, clothes, and junk, under the elevated tracks from Ueno to Okachimachi JR Station. "Motorcycle heaven," rows of showrooms, shiny machines, accessories, and parts, is northeast of Ueno JR Station along Showa-dori.
✚ L2 🚇 Ueno, Ueno-Hirokoji

DEPARTMENT STORES

The *depato* is a Japanese institution. Don't fail to visit at least one of the big ones to experience the phenomenon. The layout of the stores is easy to understand, they take credit cards, they can produce someone who speaks English, they stock almost everything, they are close to stations (they may own a line or two), and they open on Saturdays and Sundays—a big day for shopping. Closing day varies from store to store.

ISETAN
An enormous store above Shinjuku San-chome Station, with dozens of designer boutiques. The food store and restaurants are in the basement.
✚ D4 ✉ 3-14-1 Shinjuku, Shinjuku-ku ☎ 3225–2514 ◷ Thu–Tue 10–7. Closed Wed Ⓢ Shinjuku San-chome

KEIO
Above part of Shinjuku Station, with its own railway brings in the customers. See the sporting goods (4F) and kimonos (6F). Most restaurants are on 8F.
✚ D4 ✉ 1-1-4 Nishi-Shinjuku, Shinjuku-ku ☎ 3342–2111 ◷ Fri–Wed 10–7. Closed Thu Ⓢ Shinjuku

ODAKYU
Above part of Shinjuku Station, with its own railway line. Food is in the lower basement, the 11th floor has an art gallery, and restaurants are on the 14th and top floor.
✚ D4 ✉ 1-1-3 Nishi-Shinjuku, Shinjuku-ku ☎ 3342–1111 ◷ Wed–Mon 10–7. Closed Tue Ⓢ Shinjuku

MATSUYA
With bright and colorful displays, and favored by younger customers. The basement food store sells excellent box meals at sensible prices.
✚ K6 ✉ 3-6-1 Ginza, Chuo-ku ☎ 3567–1211 ◷ Mon–Wed, Fri 10–6; Sat–Sun, holidays 10–6:30. Closed Thu Ⓢ Ginza

MITSUKOSHI
Founded in the 17th century. Huge selections of toys, stationery, kimonos, and sportswear, and a fine food hall.
✚ L5 ✉ 1-7-4 Nihonbashi-Muromachi, Chuo-ku ☎ 3241–3311 ◷ Tue–Sat 10–6; Sun, holidays 10–6:30. Closed Mon Ⓢ Mitsukoshi-mae

SEIBU
With adjoining Parco fashion store and theater complex. Designer boutiques, children's wear, stationery. Top-floor restaurants. Other branches in Ikebukuro and Yurakucho.
✚ D8 ✉ 15-1 Udagawa-cho, Shibuya-ku ☎ 3462–0111 ◷ Thu–Tue 10–8:30. Closed Wed Ⓢ Shibuya

TAKASHIMAYA
Full of boutiques with famous-name designer fashions. Even the basement food store has Fauchon and Fortnum & Mason counters; both the displays and the staff are impeccably turned out.
✚ L5 ✉ 2-4-1 Nihonbashi, Chuo-ku ☎ 3211–4111 ◷ Thu–Tue 10–7. Closed Wed Ⓢ Nihonbashi
Also at:
✚ D4 ✉ Times Square, south of the station Ⓢ Shinjuku

In-store food
Department stores are a boon to visitors, and not only when they want to shop or to use the toilet facilities. Most stores have a whole selection of reasonably priced restaurants offering different food styles, normally on the top floor or in the basement. Their food departments are an eye-opener too, and an education in the ingredients of Japanese cuisine. The artistically prepared box lunches are a comparative bargain, and—if your budget is really restricted—you can taste all sorts of free samples, although they are more likely to sharpen your appetite than satisfy it.

CRAFTS & SOUVENIRS

CRAFTS

BINGO-YA
A wide choice of folk art, crafts, toys, and gifts from all parts of Japan.
➕ F3 ✉ 10-6 Wakamatsu-cho, Shinjuku-ku
☎ 3202–8778 🕐 Tue–Sun 10–7. Closed Mon
🚇 Akebonobashi (15-minute walk)

INTERNATIONAL ARCADE
Thirty shops selling crafts and souvenirs, from high quality to junk. Some antique shops.
➕ J6 ✉ 1-7-23 Uchisaiwaicho, Chiyoda-ku
☎ 3591–8668 🕐 Daily 10–6
🚇 Hibiya

JAPAN TRADITIONAL CRAFTS CENTER
Stages exhibitions and sells all sorts of arts and crafts, especially ceramics from famous Japanese potteries.
➕ F7 ✉ Plaza 246 2F, 3-1-1 Minami-Aoyama, Minato-ku
☎ 3403–2460 🕐 Fri–Wed 10–6. Closed Thu 🚇 Gaienmae

ORIENTAL BAZAAR
On Omotesando-dori, with a huge choice of handicrafts and souvenirs. Basement stalls sell bric-a-brac, dolls, kimonos.
➕ E7 ✉ 5-9-13 Jingumae, Shibuya-ku ☎ 3400–3933
🕐 Fri–Wed 9:30–6:30. Closed Thu 🚇 Omotesando

DOLLS

KYUGETSU
An old-established shop, selling traditional and many other dolls, in wood, papier-mâché, and fabric.
➕ M4 ✉ 1-20-4 Yanagibashi, Taito-ku ☎ 3861–5511
🕐 Daily 9:15–6
🚇 Asakusabashi

CERAMICS

KISSO
Fine ceramics combine traditional methods with modern designs. Shares premises with a restaurant.
➕ G7 ✉ Axis Building B1F, 5-17-1, Roppongi, Minato-ku
☎ 3582–4191 🕐 Daily 11:30–2, 5:30–9 🚇 Roppongi

KORANSHA
Fine pieces, especially the flower and bird patterns from Arita in Kyushu.
➕ K7 ✉ 5-12-12 Ginza, Chuo-ku ☎ 3543–0951
🕐 Mon–Sat 9:30–6:30. Closed Sun 🚇 Higashi-Ginza

LACQUERWARE

TOKYO LACQUERWARE
For decorative pots, cups, bowls, and boxes. Larger and finer pieces are costly.
➕ F7 ✉ 2-11-13 Minamami-Aoyama, Minato-ku
☎ 3401–5118 🕐 Mon–Fri 11–6:30; Sat 11–5. Closed Sun
🚇 Gaienmae

PAPER ART

KYUKYODO
Sells beautiful handmade papers and everything needed for calligraphy.
➕ K7 ✉ 5-7-4 Ginza, Chuo-ku ☎ 3571–4429
🕐 Daily 10–6 🚇 Higashi-Ginza

YUSHIMA NO KOBAYASHI (ORIGAMI KAIKAN)
(► 61)

Everyday quality

If the price of fine porcelain and lacquerware comes as a shock, look instead at the everyday versions sold in street markets and department stores. The Japanese sense of color and form extends to these too, and quality is usually faultless. Even the disposable baskets and boxes used for takeout meals can be minor craftworks. Special handmade and decorative papers, in the form of wrappings, stationery, boxes, dolls, fans, and *origami* designs make good gifts—light, unbreakable, and reasonably priced.

ANTIQUES, BYGONES, & JUNK

FUJI FINE ARTS

Specializing in porcelain lamps, painted screens, lacquerware, and brass.
✚ H8 ✉ Azabudai Hoei Building 1F, 2-3-20 Azabudai, Minato-ku ☎ 3582–1870 🕐 Wed–Mon 10:30–5. Closed Tue 🚇 Kamiyacho

HASEBE-YA ANTIQUES

An eclectic stock of pottery, bronze statuary, netsuke, lacquerware, and especially woodware— boxes, carvings, and furniture.
✚ G8 ✉ 1-5-24 Azabujuban, Minato-ku ☎ 3401–9998 🕐 Mon–Sat 10:30–6 🚇 Roppongi

KAMON ANTIQUES

For oriental fine art and folk art, calligraphy, and Imari ware.
✚ E8 ✉ 4-3-12 Shibuya, Shibuya-ku ☎ 3406–1765 🕐 Mon–Sat 10:30–6. Closed Sun 🚇 Shibuya

KUROFUNE ANTIQUES

A colorful and well-stocked shop, with fine porcelain, old prints, lacquerware, furniture, and folk art.
✚ G7 ✉ 7-7-4 Roppongi B1F, Minato-ku ☎ 3479–1552 🕐 Mon–Sat 10–6. Closed Sun 🚇 Roppongi

FLEA MARKETS

Sales of used goods and junk were traditionally held outside the gates of temples and shrines, and some still are. There's a tradition of settling debts before the New Year, and some people find it necessary to sell possessions. Harder times have made it more respectable to buy secondhand goods. Antiques are rare, and dealers normally latch on to them almost before the market opens. Even so, it pays to get there early, as the vendors are laying out their wares. The sales are an unusual chance to bargain: use all the skills you may have acquired elsewhere in Asia. Listings magazines (▶ 92) give details of upcoming sales. Regular sites include:

AOYAMA OVAL PLAZA

✚ E7 ✉ Near National Children's Castle, Jingumae 5-chome, Shibuya-ku 🕐 Every 3rd Sat of month 6–sunset 🚇 Omotesando

HANAZONO SHRINE

✚ E4 ✉ Opposite Marui Interior store, Shinjuku 3-chome 🕐 Every Sun 7–6 🚇 Shinjuku, Shinjuku San-chome

NOGI SHRINE

✚ G7 ✉ Roppongi, Minato-ku 🕐 Every 2nd Sun of month 7–6 🚇 Nogizaka

ROI BUILDING

✚ G7 ✉ In front of Roi Building, Roppongi 5-chome, Minato-ku 🕐 Every 4th Thu and Fri of month 7–6 🚇 Roppongi

SALVATION ARMY BAZAAR

✚ A4 ✉ 2-21-2 Wada, Suginami-ku 🕐 Every Sat 9–1 🚇 Nakano-Fujimicho (see map at station)

TOGO SHRINE

✚ E7 ✉ Harajuku, Shibuya-ku 🕐 Every 1st, 4th and 5th Sun of month 4AM–2PM 🚇 Meijijingu-mae

Collectible "antiques"

Antiques, even in the loose sense of the word as used in Japan to mean anything more than about 40 years old, are expensive. Fine pieces fetch stratospheric sums, even though the market has settled down from the 1980s' boom. Specifically Japanese collectibles include ceramics, dolls, fans, lacquerware, masks, *netsuke*, paintings, woodblock prints (*ukiyo-e*), and woodcarvings. Before exploring, look at the shops in or near the big hotels to get an idea of what is available, although their prices may be at the top of the range.

MISCELLANEOUS STORES

BOOKS

AOYAMA BOOK CENTER
Large stock of American and European titles.
➕ G8 ✉ 6-1-20 Roppongi, Minato-ku ☎ 3479–0479 🕐 Daily 10–4AM 🚇 Roppongi.
Also at:
✉ Hiroo Garden Plaza, 4-1-29 Minami-Azabu, Minato-ku

ISSEIDO
For secondhand and antique books, art books, and woodblock prints.
➕ J4 ✉ 1-7 Kanda-Jinbocho, Chiyoda-ku ☎ 3292–0071 🕐 Daily 10–7 🚇 Jinbocho

KINOKUNIYA
Close to the south exit of Shinjuku Station. The large stock of foreign books is on the 6th floor.
➕ D5 ✉ Annex Building, Times Square, 5-24-2 Sendagaya, Shibuya-ku ☎ 5361–3301 🕐 Daily 10–7 🚇 Shinjuku
Also at:
➕ D8 ✉ Tokyu Plaza, 1-2-2 Dogenzaka, Shibuya-ku

MARUZEN
A large range of imported books, travel books, and a huge number of books about every aspect of Japanese life.
➕ L5 ✉ 2-3-10 Nihonbashi, Chuo-dori ☎ 3272–7211 🕐 Mon–Sat 10–7. Closed Sun 🚇 Nihonbashi.
Also at:
Bunkamura Bookshop ➕ D8 ✉ B1F, 2-24-1 Dogenzaka, Shibuya-ku

OHYA-SHOBO
Several secondhand book and print stores are clustered together along the road heading east from the station. This one has antique illustrated books and fine prints.
➕ J4 ✉ 1-2 Kanda-Jinbocho, Chiyoda-ku ☎ 3291–0062 🕐 Daily 10–7 🚇 Jinbocho

SANSEIDO
A general bookstore with a large English section.
➕ D8 ✉ Tokyu Bunka Kaikan 5F, 2-21-12 Shibuya, Shibuya-ku ☎ 3407–4545 🕐 Daily 10–7 🚇 Shibuya
Also at:
➕ D4 ✉ Odakyu department store, 1-1-3 Nishi-Shinjuku, Shinjuku-ku 🕐 Wed–Mon 10–7. Closed Tue 🚇 Shinjuku

PEARLS

MIKIMOTO
This is the big name in the field of cultured pearls, with a prime location and top prices.
➕ K6 ✉ 4-5-5 Ginza, Chuo-ku ☎ 3535–4611 🕐 Thu–Tue 10–6. Closed Wed 🚇 Ginza

TASAKI PEARL
This store has several showrooms, and offers tours and demonstrations. City tour buses often include a visit.
➕ H7 ✉ 1-3-3 Akasaka, Minato-ku ☎ 5561–8880 🕐 Daily 9–6:30 🚇 Akasaka

HOBBIES & HOME IMPROVEMENTS

TOKYU HANDS
Eight floors are packed with everything you need for model-making, plus car maintenance, painting, carpentry and more.
➕ D8 ✉ 12–18 Udagawa-cho, Shibuya-ku ☎ 5489–5111 🕐 Daily 10–7 🚇 Shibuya
Also at:
➕ D5 ✉ Times Square, near Shinjuku Station 🚇 Shinjuku

High fashion
The elegant young *oeru* (➤ 7, panel) in search of the latest designs patrols the fashion boutiques, which are conveniently clustered in "vertical malls." You can see her in action at:

Bell Commons
➕ F7 ✉ 2-14-6 Kita-Aoyama, Minato-ku 🕐 Daily 11–8 🚇 Gaienmae

La Forêt
➕ E7 ✉ 1-11-16 Jingumae, Shibuya-ku 🕐 Daily 10:30–7 🚇 Meijijingu-mae

From 1st Building
➕ F7 ✉ 5-3-10 Minami-Aoyama, Minato-ku 🕐 Daily 10:30–7 🚇 Omotesando

ELECTRICAL GOODS, CAMERAS, & MUSIC

ELECTRICAL GOODS

Don't expect any real bargains. Prices may be higher than in the US, even for Japanese-made products. If your itinerary includes Hong Kong, you will certainly do better to buy there, but it is still fascinating to see the range on offer in Japan, and the local marketing methods. Tell the sales staff where you are from, so that you get the right specification of equipment: they cater for all markets.

LAOX

A giant electrical retailer whose building even looks like a huge VCR standing on end. The duty-free branch is nearby at 1-13-3 Soto-Kanda. They also sell toys and even pearls.
🕂 L3 ✉ 1-2-9 Soto-Kanda, Chiyoda-ku ☎ 3253–7111 🕙 Mon–Sat 10–7:45; Sun 10–7:15 🚇 Akihabara 🚆 Akihabara (JR)

MINAMI

Five floors packed with electrical equipment, plus a surprising sixth floor of imported furniture, including antiques.
🕂 L3 ✉ 4-3-3 Soto-Kanda, Chiyoda-ku ☎ 3255–3173 🕙 Daily 9–5:30 🚇 Akihabara 🚆 Akihabara (JR)

YAMAGIWA

From light bulbs to satellite dishes, this is one of the biggest retailers in Akihabara.
🕂 L3 ✉ 4-1-1 Soto-Kanda, Chiyoda-ku ☎ 3253–2111 🕙 Sun–Thu 10–5:30; Fri–Sat 10–8 🚇 Akihabara 🚆 Akihabara (JR)

PHOTOGRAPHIC EQUIPMENT

New means expensive, but since the Japanese photographer must have the latest, there is a lot of secondhand gear available at a more sensible price.

SAKURAYA

Not only cameras and film, but video equipment and electronics galore.
🕂 D4 ✉ 3-26-10 Shinjuku, Shinjuku-ku ☎ 3352–4711 🕙 Daily 10–8 🚇 Shinjuku

YODOBASHI CAMERA

Near the west exit of Shinjuku Station. A glitzy, multilevel, noisy, and crowded store full of every sort of equipment and film. There's another branch east of the station.
🕂 D4 ✉ 1-11-1 Nishi-Shinjuku, Shinjuku-ku ☎ 3346–1010 🕙 Daily 9:30–9:30 🚇 Shinjuku

MUSIC TAPES & CDS

TOWER RECORDS

One of the world's biggest retailers, with eight floors stocking every style of recorded music.
🕂 D7 ✉ 1-22-14 Jinnan, Shibuya-ku ☎ 3340–3581 🕙 Daily 10–10 🚇 Shibuya

VIRGIN MEGASTORE

Tens of thousands of CDs, cassettes, and videos are in stock. The dozens of listening stations are often not enough for the crowds of buyers.
🕂 E4 ✉ Marui Fashion Building B1F, 3-30-16 Shinjuku, Shinjuku-ku ☎ 3353–0056 🕙 Daily 10–7 🚇 Shinjuku San-chome

Akihabara

Follow signs from the subway or JR station west to "Akihabara Electric Town," where several blocks of multistory emporia are stuffed with everything from electronic marvels to workaday washing machines. Smaller stores specialize in computer software, mobile phones, speaker systems, and even humble switches and cables. Goods flow out onto the street; sound systems are at pain threshhold. A lot of signs are in Russian, seeming to indicate that the vendors have identified a new market. Carry your passport to benefit from duty-free concessions, and ask for discounts on any pretext you can think of.

JAPANESE THEATER & ARTS

People's theater

Kabuki developed under the Tokugawa *shoguns*, and two prohibitions gave it the character is still has today. In 1629, women were banned from the stage, resulting in the tradition of *onnegata*—male actors specializing in female roles. Then it was forbidden to attend the plays wearing swords. The *samurai* class, who wouldn't be seen in public without a sword, stayed away, and *kabuki* became an entertainment for the masses. The plays blend historical romance, tragedy and comedy, music, dance, and acrobatics, performed in vivid costumes and make-up.

KABUKI

The Kabuki-za Theater is a Ginza landmark. Full programs last four to five hours, including two intervals; tickets cost upwards of ¥2,500 (¥10,000 for good seats). Recognizing that foreigners will not want to spend that much time or money watching an incomprehensible spectacle, no matter how colorful, the theater offers two special arrangements. You can see a one-act play, up to an hour long, for about ¥800 for a non-reservable, distant 4th-floor seat. Or you can rent an English-language "Earphone Guide," synchronized to the action, but only available with the full-price seats.

KABUKI-ZA THEATER
✚ K7 ✉ 4-12-15 Ginza, Chuo-ku ☎ 3541–3131 🚇 Higashi-Ginza

NATIONAL THEATER (KOKORITSU GEJIKO)
✚ H5 ✉ 4-1 Hayabusa-cho, Chiyoda-ku ☎ 3265–7411 🚇 Hanzomon

NOH

Much more ancient than *kabuki*, infinitely stylized, and performed by masked actors, *noh* is less accessible still to foreigners. Even the Japanese confess to wishing it didn't go on so long, and so slowly. The younger generation says "*Noh*? No!" But look in listings magazines (➤ 92) for open-air, torch-lit performances at temples, where even the uninitiated can enjoy the gorgeous costumes and setting. A regular indoor venue is:

KANZE NOH-GAKUDO
✚ D8 ✉ 1-16-4 Shoto, Shibuya-ku ☎ 3469–5241 🚇 Shibuya

BUNRAKU

In this form of puppet theater, near-lifesize figures are worked by three puppeteers, while narrators tell the stories to a musical accompaniment. Like *noh*, it is an esoteric art for which few foreigners acquire a taste. Performances are sometimes staged at the National Theater (see above).

BONSAI

By artfully snipping roots and pruning branches, a tree sapling can be kept to a miniature scale while reaching maturity. The aim is to produce a specimen which looks natural in every way, except size. Some prized examples, gnarled and apparently windswept, have been handed down for over 200 years. Department stores and shops all over Tokyo sell the little trees in all price ranges. Check on import regulations before trying to take one home.

IKEBANA

The art of flower arranging developed in parallel with the tea ceremony to decorate the room in a simple but exquisite fashion. The Tourist Information Center (➤ 91) can tell you about classes.

MUSIC & FILM

CLASSICAL MUSIC

Japanese soloists and conductors have taken the world by storm, and standards of performance in Tokyo are excellent. Many foreign soloists, orchestras, and opera companies also appear. Ticket prices are high (¥3,000–¥25,000). Among the many concert halls are:

BUNKAMURA ORCHARD HALL

Part of an impressive cultural center, with a theater and cinemas.
✚ D8 ✉ 2-24-1 Dogenzaka, Shibuya-ku ☎ 3477–9999
🚇 Shibuya

SUNTORY HALL

A fine new concert hall in the Ark Hills development.
✚ H7 ✉ 1-13-1 Akasaka, Minato-ku ☎ 3505–1001
🚇 Kamiyacho

TOKYO METROPOLITAN FESTIVAL HALL (TOKYO BUNKA KAIKAN)

Located at the entrance to Ueno Park. Seats 2,300 in the main hall, 700 in a smaller auditorium.
✚ L2 ✉ 5-45 Ueno Koen, Taito-ku ☎ 3828–2111
🚇 Ueno

JAZZ

Many local and touring musicians appear in Roppongi and Harajuku clubs. Blue Note Tokyo seems to book the biggest visiting names but ticket prices are expensive, starting at ¥8,000. Check the listings magazines (➤ 92) to see who is in town.

BLUE NOTE TOKYO

✚ E7 ✉ 5-13-3 Minami-Aoyama, Minato-ku
☎ 3407–5781
🚇 Omotesando

POP & ROCK CONCERTS

Local and visiting stars perform at the Tokyo Dome (➤ 82), and on summer evenings outdoors in Hibiya Park (➤ 40). Another indoor venue is:

NIPPON BUDOKAN HALL

✚ J4 ✉ 2-3 Kitanomaru Koen, Chiyoda-ku
☎ 3216–5100 🚇 Kudanshita

FILM

Japan's directors made a name for themselves in the 1950s and 60s but Tokyo now has a much bigger appetite for foreign movies than for its own. Most come from Hollywood, shown with the original soundtracks and Japanese subtitles. Fitting the local pattern of early close-down, the last show begins at about 7PM (later on Friday and Saturday). Smaller "boutique" cinemas screen later performances and provide an infinitely varied diet, including classics, reruns, and European films. Tickets are around ¥2,000. For a little more money you can reserve seats. Movie listings can be found in the monthly *Tokyo Journal*.

Central ticket agencies

For most theaters, concert halls, and major sports arenas, you can reserve tickets up to the day before the performance at agencies such as:

Kyukyodo
✚ K7 ✉ 5-7-4 Ginza, Chuo-ku ☎ 3571–0401
🚇 Higashi-Ginza

Play Guide Honten
✚ K6 ✉ 2-6-4 Ginza, Chuo-ku ☎ 3561–8821
🚇 Ginza

On the day of the performance, telephone the venue and arrange to collect the tickets there; if you have a problem making yourself understood, ask someone at your hotel to make the call.

ENTERTAINMENT DISTRICTS

"Like calls to like" is the Japanese equivalent of "birds of a feather," and it certainly applies to Tokyo's nightspots. The crowds go where the action is, so ever more places open up in these areas in order to tap the market.

AKASAKA

Two parallel streets, Hitotsugi-dori and Tamachi-dori, and the narrow alleyways between them are packed with bars, clubs, and restaurants. It's respectable and rather expensive, although not quite in the Ginza league, and mostly frequented by company men on expense accounts and people staying at the area's big hotels.

GINZA

The prices in the clubs and top restaurants are legendary, and prohibitive for anyone not on an unlimited expense account. Others can enjoy the street scene, find a fast food or budget restaurant, and enjoy a drink in one of the affordable bars or big beer halls.

ROPPONGI

This is a favorite with Tokyo's younger foreign contingent as well as more adventurous Japanese, partly because it's still awake at 4AM, while elsewhere has quieted down by midnight. The Almond coffee house at the main street crossing near the subway station is a popular rendezvous and landmark. There's a huge choice of eating and drinking places nearby, but prices have risen in recent years to rival Akasaka levels. Aggressive drunken foreigners are a problem in a few of the lower-priced bars and discos.

SHIBUYA

Busy and cheerful, with a mainly young crowd, this is less sleazy than Kabukicho, more Japanese than Roppongi, and not as expensive as Akasaka. There's a host of fast-food outlets and a wide choice of ethnic restaurants. Local groups play in the live music bars.

SHINJUKU

As the gateway to the city from the west, Shinjuku has always entertained travelers. The railway gave it a boost, and Kabukicho northeast of the station became Japan's biggest red-light district. The name came from a planned *kabuki* theater. This was never built, but the big Koma Theater is a landmark. From respectable bars and fine restaurants, the nightlife runs the range, testing the limits of legality. Women in vinyl miniskirts hand out packets of tissues printed with addresses and prices of massage parlors; hard-faced barkers urge passers-by in to see strip shows, peep shows, and bottomless bars. These venues are only for the broadminded prepared to forget the human exploitation and the Yakuza (local Mafia) who control a lot of this activity.

Meeting point

Everyone in Tokyo knows the statue of Hachiko, an Akita dog who used to walk with his master, a university professor, to Shibuya Station each morning, and meet him off the train again in the evening. One day in 1925, the professor did not return: he had suddenly been taken ill and died. Hachiko waited for the last train and then sadly made his way home. For seven years, he came every evening to wait, until at last he too died. Touched by such loyalty, the people of Tokyo paid for the bronze statue outside the station.

OTHER IDEAS

A night out can be costly, unless you are being entertained by local business contacts, who will expect to pick up the bill (you can return the hospitality when they visit your home country). You are not likely to be invited to a Japanese home until you know someone very well; anyway most people eat out more than they do at home.

LOCAL CHOICES

Robatayaki restaurants are cheerful, noisy places where varied foods are cooked on an open grill amid clouds of smoke. A *ryori-ya* or *shokudo* is a mixed-menu restaurant: plastic replicas in the window show the choices and prices. *Chuka ryori-ya* are basic Chinese restaurants serving such staples as fried rice and noodle dishes. *Ramen-ya* and *soba-ya* serve inexpensive bowls of noodles in a soup or with a topping. A *kissaten* is a coffee house serving light snacks and sweet pastries —the coffee may be expensive but you can sit as long as you like. For a moderately priced breakfast of toast, coffee, a boiled egg, and small salad, ask for *maningu sabisu* (morning service).

BARS

The variety is endless. Take a look inside and decide if the atmosphere appeals to you. If prices are not posted, ask for a list. Bottles of good French or Australian wine start from about ¥2,000. Beers run from ¥500 to ¥800 or more. The good, if rather bland, local whiskey costs much less than imported brands. Bars and clubs where local or Western groups perform ("live houses") generally make an extra charge of ¥1,000–1,500. A *nomi-ya* is an informal neighborhood bar, also known as *akachochin*, and indicated by the red lantern outside. *Karaoke* bars have spread round the world like an infection but this is where the idea of amateur singing to a tape was born. Unless you want to fork out a large fee (¥5,000 an hour is typical), avoid bars where a hostess sits with you while you have an outrageously expensive drink (in less legitimate places other services can be negotiated).

DISCOS

These are concentrated mainly in Shibuya, Shinjuku, and especially Roppongi where the Square Building alone houses discos on most of its ten floors. It is impossible to predict from day to day which will be jumping and which empty, or closed for good. Ask local contacts and check the listings magazines (▶ 92). A cover charge of about ¥4,000 usually includes a couple of drink tickets. The downside of the disco scene is the growth of liquor-induced aggressive behavior, and it's almost always foreigners who are to blame. When the atmosphere turns nasty, it is best to leave and find somewhere else.

Beer halls

These big, informal places, vaguely modeled on German *bierkeller*, are mostly run by the brewery companies. You sit at large or small tables, or bar counters, and order beers and plates of savory snacks—three or four would add up to a meal.

Beer Station Sapporo
✚ E10 ✉ Yebisu Garden Place, 3 Ebisu, Shibuya-ku
Ⓔ Ebisu

Flamme d'Or Asahi
✚ N2 ✉ Asahi Brewery, 1 Azumabashi, Sumida-ku
Ⓔ Asakusa

Kirin City
✚ K6 ✉ Bunshodo Building 2F, 3-4-12 Ginza, Chuo-ku
Ⓔ Ginza

Many department stores turn their roofs into beer gardens during the sultry summer months.

SPORTS & SPORTING VENUES

Big stars

In the past, few foreigners ever undertook the rigorous training, let alone reached the senior ranks of *sumo*, but the picture changed in the late 1980s when the Hawaiian Konishiki was a frequent winner. Then came the Irish-Polynesian Akebono, who became the sole *yokozuna* (grand champion). The Japanese tolerated the invasion, while hoping for a home-grown hero, so there was relief at the promotion of Takanohana to *yokozuna* rank in 1994. Television has made *sumo* stars into national figures. Most of the training stables are in Ryogoku, and some permit visitors to watch morning practice sessions, between 5 and 10:30AM. Have a Japanese speaker make an appointment for you.

Azumazeki Stable
☎ 3625–0033
Kazugano Stable
☎ 3631–1871

SUMO

Literally "fat power," this form of wrestling was originally practiced at Shinto shrines. Matches are still surrounded by time-honored ceremonial. After purification and other rituals, the two huge contenders collide, each intent on unbalancing the other and tipping him over or forcing him from the ring. Tournaments (*basho*) are scheduled in January, May, and September. Tickets for good seats are expensive, although they include a good boxed meal. Bouts are televised from 4 to 6PM each day of the tournament. The main Tokyo venue is:

KOKUGIKAN SUMO HALL
✚ N4 ✉ 1-3-28 Yokoami, Sumida-ku ☎ 3623–5111
🕐 10–6 (main bouts 3–6)
🚋 Ryogoku (JR)

BASEBALL

This is the prime claimant to the title of national sport—top players and managers become media superstars. Most Japanese have probably forgotten where it originated. Tokyo has several teams in the two major leagues and often provides the winner of the Japan Series play-off. The season is from April to October, and the main venue is:

TOKYO DOME (KORAKUEN)
✚ J3 ✉ 1-3-61 Koraku, Bunkyo-ku ☎ 3811–2111
🚋 Suidobashi

GOLF

Half of Tokyo's businessmen claim to play, but the game is expensive and the courses too remote for most of them to indulge regularly. They console themselves at driving ranges, whose big net cages are a feature of the skyline.

TENNIS

Some of the bigger hotels have courts, even in Tokyo itself as well as at the Tokyo Bay resorts. So does Hibiya Park (➤ 40) downtown.

SWIMMING

The nearest reasonably clean beach is at Kamakura (➤ 20), which is crowded—especially on weekends—from June to the end of August, and deserted the rest of the year. Toshima-en amusement park (➤ 62, panel) has several swimming pools; Yoyogi Park's sports center (➤ 31) has a large one, but it's often in use for events. Hotel pools are for residents or members of their health clubs.

PLACES TO JOG

Traffic congestion and the lack of sidewalks make the streets a less than enjoyable place to jog, but there's a park within easy reach of most hotels. Best of all is the Imperial Palace Garden (➤ 36). Many big hotels will give guests jogging maps.

BATH HOUSES

The earth's crust seems especially thin in Japan. The unstable ground threatens disaster in the form of earthquakes and *tsunami*, but there's compensation in the countless hot springs. Tokyo is no exception. Coffee-colored, mineral-rich water from beneath the city is piped to dozens of *onsen* (hot spring-fed baths); other public baths are called *sento*. They traditionally served as community centers where local people gathered to relax, and in older parts of the city they still do. These days, the sexes are generally segregated: only in some open-air rural spas is there mixed bathing. Three traditional *onsen* are:

ASAKUSA KANNON ONSEN

A large and very hot bath esteemed for its curative properties.

➕ N2 ✉ Asakusa 2-chome, Taito-ku ☎ 3844–4141
🕐 Daily 6:30AM–6:30PM
Ⓜ Asakusa

AZABU JUBAN KASHINOYU

A cozy *onsen* on the third floor of a modern building.

➕ G8 ✉ 1-5-22 Azabu Juban, Minato-ku ☎ 3401–8324
🕐 Wed–Mon 3–11. Closed Tue
Ⓜ Roppongi

MIKOKO YU

Very hot natural spring and therapeutic herbal baths.

➕ Off map ✉ 3-30-8 Ishihara, Sumida-ku
☎ 3623–1695 🕐 Tue–Sun 4PM–midnight. Closed Mon
Ⓜ Hunjo– Azumabashi (Asakusa Line)

ORDER OF THE BATH

● On entering, take off all your clothes in the locker room.
● Take only your towel, soap, and shampoo into the bath room.
● Sit on one of the stools provided, well away from the bath.
● Douse yourself with water using a scoop, bucket, or shower, whatever is provided.
● Wash thoroughly all over and meticulously rinse off all the soap. *No trace of soap must get into the bath itself.*
● Immerse yourself gradually in the bath (*ofuro*). If there's a choice try the less hot bath first. Temperatures typically range from 42°C (108°F) up to about 48°C (118°F).
● Don't put your head under the water.
● If you feel dizzy get out.
● Some users recommend getting in and out several times.
● Don't drink alcohol before the bath.

If you're staying in a private house, much the same rules apply. Replace the cover on the bath to keep the water hot for other users. In a *ryokan* (▶ 86), which may have a bath for couples or families as well as the men's and women's, the maid will usually ask you when you would like to take your bath, and come to let you know when it is ready. The accepted bath time in a *ryokan* or private home is before the evening meal.

Sacred and profane

Bathing has a spiritual as well as a social dimension: the Shinto code emphasizes purity and cleanliness, not only of the mind but of the body. Faith and medical research agree that a hot, deep bath is beneficial to health, reducing stress and tension and relieving aches and pains.

"Soaplando" massage parlors are less concerned with the spiritual element, though they might claim to be relieving stress. Concentrated in Kabukicho (▶ 80), these places take their name from the way the masseuses coat their bodies and the client's with lather before getting to work.

83

LUXURY HOTELS ($$$)

What you pay for

The cost of a double room per night, with private bath (except for *ryokan* and hostels), excluding breakfast, is shown by the symbols:

$$$ = over ¥24,000
$$ = ¥12,000–24,000
$ = under ¥12,000

Tokyo deserves its reputation for high prices, but the top hotels are no more expensive than the equivalent in New York, London, or Frankfurt. Take into account the standard of service, facilities, and impeccable cleanliness and they might be thought good value. Almost all Japanese hotels provide toothbrushes, toothpaste, a razor and shaving cream, and a cotton *yukata*, robe, or pajamas.

AKASAKA PRINCE

The 40-story curved building stands out on its hilltop site, close to Akasaka and a short subway ride from Ginza. Acres of marble, 761 rooms, 12 restaurants, shops, and business services.

➕ H6 ✉ 1-2 Kioi-cho, Chiyoda-ku ☎ 3234–1111. Fax 3262–5163 🚇 Nagatacho

ANA HOTEL TOKYO

In the Ark Hills area, between Roppongi and Akasaka, a 37-story, 903-room block with a sober exterior and lots of marble inside. Health club and pool, executive floor, and several restaurants.

➕ H7 ✉ 1-12-33 Akasaka, Minato-ku ☎ 3505–1111. Fax 3505–1155 🚇 Akasaka

IMPERIAL

A city-within-a-city, in the heart of Ginza and facing Hibiya Park. 1,059 rooms, over 20 restaurants, dozens of shops, a health club, and a pool. Rooms are beautifully appointed, with superb views from the upper stories.

➕ J6 ✉ 1-1-1 Uchisaiwaicho, Chiyoda-ku ☎ 3504–1111. Fax 3581–9146 🚇 Hibiya

OKURA

Stately, formal, one of the first of the postwar grand hotels, with 858 rooms, many restaurants, an art gallery, and indoor and outdoor pools.

➕ H7 ✉ 2-10-4 Toranomon, Minato-ku ☎ 3582–0111. Fax 3582–3707 🚇 Toranomon

PALACE

Overlooks the moats of the Imperial Palace. A subway stop from Ginza. Elegant public areas and 393 beautifully appointed guest rooms.

➕ K5 ✉ 1-1-1 Marunouchi, Chiyoda-ku ☎ 3211–5211. Fax 3211–6987 🚇 Otemachi

PARK HYATT TOKYO

On the 39th to 52nd floors of a pyramid-topped glass tower at the western edge of Shinjuku. Elegant and spacious, with 178 rooms, three restaurants, and a rooftop swimming pool.

➕ C5 ✉ 3-7-1-2 Nishi-Shinjuku, Shinjuku-ku ☎ 5322–1234. Fax 5322–1288 🚇 Shinjuku

ROPPONGI PRINCE

Compact 216-room hotel close to Roppongi. Courtyard with a café and swimming pool.

➕ H7 ✉ 3-2-7 Roppongi, Minato-ku ☎ 3587–1111. Fax 3587–0770 🚇 Roppongi

TOKYO HILTON INTERNATIONAL

One of Shinjuku's high-rises: great views from the upper floors. 807 rooms, 5 restaurants, indoor and outdoor pools, and tennis courts.

➕ C4 ✉ 6-6-2 Nishi-Shinjuku, Shinjuku-ku ☎ 3344–5111. Fax 3342–6094 🚇 Shinjuku

WESTIN TOKYO

A stylish hotel with richly decorated public areas and 444 guest rooms, part of a new development on the former Sapporo Brewery site.

➕ E10 ✉ Yebisu Garden Place, 1-4-1 Mita, Meguro-ku ☎ 5423–7000. Fax 5423–7600 🚇 Ebisu

MID-RANGE HOTELS ($$)

ALCYONE
This small hotel (74 rooms) offers a friendly, personal service. It is located close to central Ginza's nightlife and shopping.
⊕ K6 ✉ 4-14-3 Ginza, Chuo-ku ☎ 3541–3621. Fax 3541–3263 Ⓢ Higashi-Ginza

GINZA CAPITAL
A basic business hotel with compact rooms, close to Tsukiji subway station, reasonably convenient for Ginza.
⊕ L7 ✉ 2-1-4 Tsukiji, Chuo-ku ☎ 3543–8211. Fax 3543–7839 Ⓢ Tsukiji

IBIS
A business hotel with more than average style, and located close to the Roppongi entertainment district.
⊕ G7 ✉ 7-14-4 Roppongi, Minato-ku ☎ 3403–4411. Fax 3479–0609 Ⓢ Roppongi

SHIBA DAIMON
Few Western guests; good Chinese resataurant. Located in the Tokyo Tower area.
⊕ J8 ✉ 2-3-6 Shiba-Daimon, Minato-ku ☎ 3431–3716. Fax 3434–5177 Ⓢ Daimon

SHINJUKU WASHINGTON
This shiny modern business hotel, near the Shinjuku skyscrapers, has 1,633 compact rooms and provides largely impersonal or automated services. Five minutes' walk from Shinjuku Station.
⊕ D5 ✉ 3-2-9 Nishi-Shinjuku, Shinjuku-ku ☎ 3343–3111. Fax 3342–2575 Ⓢ Shinjuku

STAR
A small, functional but pleasant hotel with 80 rooms, only a couple of minutes' walk from Shinjuku Station and the entertainment district.
⊕ D4 ✉ 7-10-5 Nishi-Shinjuku, Shinjuku-ku ☎ 3361–1111. Fax 3369–4216 Ⓢ Shinjuku

SUN HOTEL SHINBASHI
A central area business hotel, three minutes' walk from Shinbashi JR or subway stations, one stop away from central Ginza.
⊕ J7 ✉ 3-5-2 Shinbashi, Minato-ku ☎ 3591–3351. Fax 3592–1977 Ⓢ Shinbashi

SUN ROUTE SHIBUYA
An efficient, modern 182-room business hotel, one of a Japan-wide chain. Only five minutes' walk from the station and lively center of Shibuya.
⊕ D8 ✉ 1-11 Nanpeidaimachi, Shibuya-ku ☎ 3464–6411. Fax 3464–1678 Ⓢ Shibuya

TOKYO CITY HOTEL
A typical business hotel in the heart of Nihonbashi, three stops from Ginza by subway.
⊕ L5 ✉ 1-5-4 Nihonbashi-honcho, Chuo-ku ☎ 3270–7671. Fax 3270–8930 Ⓢ Mitsukoshimae

TOKYO STATION HOTEL
An old-fashioned hotel in part of the historic station building. Central but with few facilities.
⊕ K5 ✉ 1-9-1 Marunouchi, Chiyoda-ku ☎ 3231–2511. Fax 3231–3513 Ⓢ Tokyo

The bare essentials
Most places in the mid-range category are "business hotels," providing a small room and tiny bathroom, telephone and TV, perhaps an in-house restaurant, and little else. The main difference between these and other hotels is location. The relatively high price reflects the cost of land, rents, and labor, not the minimal facilities.

Hotel pass
The Japan Hotel Pass, bought from travel agents, gives a good discount on room rates at a dozen or so hotels in Tokyo, but you must reserve rooms at the time of purchase. This and other conditions have to be balanced against the price advantage.

BUDGET ACCOMMODATIONS

When all else fails...

Capsule hotels provide a modern version of bunk beds: stacked boxes, often likened to coffins. At about 3 feet x 3 feet x 6 feet, they are slightly larger than conventional bunk beds, but are not for sufferers of claustrophobia. They're for men only, mainly those who have partied too long and missed the last train home.

"**Love hotels**" give couples—including married couples—a chance to be alone together. During the day and evening, rooms are rented by the hour, or two. After 10PM an economy all-night rate applies. Look for a gaudily lit desert castle or Roman villa just off the main streets of Shibuya, Ikebukuro, East Shinjuku, or Roppongi. The rooms can be elaborately decorated; photos of them are proudly displayed at the entrance.

ASIA CENTER OF JAPAN ($)

A rare budget hotel, with 172 plain, Western-style rooms, some with a private bathroom. Cafeteria. Reserve well in advance.
H7 ✉ 8-10-32 Akasaka, Minato-ku ☎ 3402–6111. Fax 3402–0738
Ⓜ Aoyamaitchome

YMCA ASIA YOUTH CENTER ($$)

Both sexes are welcome. Rooms have private bathrooms. Seven or eight minutes' walk from Suidobashi or Jinbocho stations.
J3 ✉ 2-5-5 Saragakucho, Chiyoda-ku ☎ 3233–0611. Fax 3233–0633 Ⓜ Suidobashi

YWCA SADOWARA ($$)

Very small but pleasant, so early reservation is essential. A few rooms for couples (M/F or F/F) are available. A few minutes' walk from Ichigaya station.
G4 ✉ 3-1-1 Ichigaya-Sadoharacho, Shinjuku-ku ☎ 3268–7313. Fax 3268–4452 Ⓜ Ichigaya

RYOKAN

These traditional Japanese lodgings can be very expensive and reluctant to take foreigners. In Tokyo the JNTO suggests a few that welcome tourists and are reasonably priced. Rooms normally have *tatami* (mats) and futon bedding (a thin mattress and quilt) which is rolled up until evening; a few have Western-style rooms too.

KIMI RYOKAN ($)

A friendly little place with Japanese-style rooms; it is popular with Westerners and often full. Seven minutes' walk northwest of Ikebukuro Station.
Off map ✉ 2-36-8 Ikebukuro, Toshima-ku ☎ 3971–3766 Ⓜ Ikebukuro

SAKURA RYOKAN ($)

Close to Ueno and Asakusa, with Western- and Japanese-style rooms.
M1 ✉ 2-6-2 Iriya, Taito-ku ☎ 3876–8118. Fax 3873–9456 Ⓜ Iriya

SAWANOYA RYOKAN

A traditional inn with 12 rooms, close to Ueno Park in the old Yanaka neighborhood.
K1 ✉ 2-3-11 Yanaka, Taito-ku ☎ 3822–2251. Fax 3822–2252 Ⓜ Nezu

HOSTELS

Expensive by international standards, hostels are nevertheless often full. Try to reserve well in advance, although it may be worth telephoning at the last moment. There's no age restriction, but if you don't belong to any YHA you may be charged extra.

TOKYO KOKUSAI (INTERNATIONAL) YOUTH HOSTEL ($)

Simple accommodations in a modern high-rise. Reservations in advance are required. Send a letter with a self-addressed postcard for reply.
H3 ✉ Central Plaza 18F, 2-1-1 Kaguragashi, Shinjuku-ku ☎ 3235–1107. Fax 3267–4000 Ⓜ Iidabashi

TOKYO
travel facts

ARRIVING & DEPARTING

Before you go

- All visitors must have a passport.
- Citizens of the UK, Republic of Ireland, and Germany do not need a visa for stays of up to 180 days.
- Citizens of the USA, Canada, Netherlands, and New Zealand may stay 90 days without a visa.
- Australian and South African citizens can obtain a free visa from Japanese embassies or consulates.
- No inoculations are required.

When to go

- Spring brings plum, peach, and cherry blossom, October through November the golden colors of the fall; but these seasons are also peak holiday times for the Japanese.

Climate

- Summers are hot and humid.
- The rainiest months are June and mid-September to October.
- Spring and autumn are warm.
- Winters are quite dry and not excessively cold. The days are usually brisk and bright.

Arriving by air

- Narita, Tokyo's international airport is 40 miles northeast of the city.
- Airport Limousine and Airport Shuttle coaches run to Tokyo City Air Terminal (TCAT) or to major hotels.
- JR trains connect the airport with Tokyo Station; Keisei Railway trains link it to Ueno and Higashi-Ginza stations.
- Buses cost about ¥3,000 and take from 70 minutes to 2 hours.
- Train fares cost ¥1,000 – ¥3,000 for the quickest (57 minutes).
- Don't take a taxi: the fare would be at least ¥22,000.

- Tokyo's older airport, Haneda (12 miles south of the city), is used by domestic flights and China Airlines flights to and from Taiwan. A monorail connects it to Hamamatsu-cho Station on the JR Yamanote Line.

Customs regulations

- Duty-free allowances are 200 cigarettes or 50 cigars, 3 x 750ml bottles of liquor, 2oz perfume, ¥200,000 worth of gifts. A green-route system operates.

Airport tax

- Airport tax, for international departures only, is ¥2,040 (¥1,020 for ages 2–11).

ESSENTIAL FACTS

Travel insurance

- Check your insurance coverage before your trip; if necessary, buy a travel policy to cover against loss or theft of belongings, travel delays, and medical costs (including repatriation).

Opening hours

- Shops: Mon–Sat 10–6, 7 or 8.
- Banks: Mon–Fri 9–3.
- Offices: Mon–Fri 9–5 (businesses work half day on Sat).
- Museums: Tue–Sun 10, 10:30 or 11–4 or 5. (Closed Tue if Mon a national holiday.)

National holidays

- If a national hoiday falls on a Sunday, the Monday following is taken as a holiday.
- January: 1 (New Year's Day); 15 (Coming of Age Day for 20-year-olds).
- February: 11 (Foundation Day).
- March: 20 or 21 (Vernal Equinox Day).

- April: 29 (Greenery Day).
- May: 3 (Constitution Day);
  4 (National Holiday);
  5 (Children's Day).
- September: 15 (Respect for the Aged Day); 23 or 24 (Autumn Equinox Day).
- October: 10 (Health in Sports Day).
- November: 3 (Culture Day); 23 (Labor Day).
- December: 23 (Emperor's Birthday).

Money matters

- The unit of currency is the yen (¥). Coins in use are ¥1, 5, 10, 50, 100, 500. Banknotes are for ¥1,000, 5,000, and 10,000.
- Traveler's checks in yen may be used instead of cash. Those in other currencies can be changed at banks or at hotels, where the exchange rate may not be quite as good. A passport is needed.
- Major credit cards are accepted by most hotels, big stores, and many restaurants, but rarely by smaller ones or fast-food outlets. It is still essential, and safe, to carry cash. Telephones and ticket-vending machines take 10, 50, and 100 yen coins.
- ATMs outside banks will take some cards. Check with card issuers to see which are accepted.

Etiquette

- Japanese custom is to bow when meeting someone. How deeply to bow is a subtle matter of age and status which you are not expected to understand. A handshake will be accepted, but an attempt to follow custom will be appreciated.
- When visiting a Japanese home, bring a present, ideally something unusual from your own country, as beautifully wrapped as possible. Do not expect it to be opened in

your presence. You will probably receive something in return, at a later date.

- Shoes must be removed before entering a home, a *ryokan*, many shrine halls, and some restaurants. Slippers are usually provided, but it will save embarrassment if your socks are free from holes.
- Visiting cards are exchanged at every opportunity. If you are on business, take a large supply. They should state your position in your organization. If possible, have a translation in Japanese characters printed on the reverse. Hotels can arrange this quickly. When given a card, study it with interest; do not put it away unread.
- For table etiquette ➤ 65, panel.
- It is not usual to tip in Japan, except for special extra services. A 10–15 percent service charge is added to hotel and some restaurant checks. Porters charge a set fee.

Lone travelers

- Tokyo need not present problems for female visitors.
- The streets and subways are safe.

Places of worship

- Weekend English-language newspapers and *Yellow Pages* (in English), available in most hotels, list all main denominations with addresses and phone numbers.

Student travelers

- An international student card will reduce admission charges at museums and other attractions.
- There is a shortage of budget accommodations, but the JNTO helps and publishes lists.

Time differences

- Japan is on GMT plus 9 (UTC plus 9), all year round.

Restrooms
- Hotels have the Western type; some have heated seats and even an optional "paperless" mode with warm water jets and hot air to clean and dry your underside.
- The Japanese version, in most public lavatories, is at ground level with no seat. You squat over it, facing the flushing handle. Carry your own paper.
- Department stores usually have both versions. Not all public toilets are segregated.

Electricity
- 100V AC, 50Hz. US 110V equipment will operate. Plugs have two flat, parallel pins.

Finding an address
- Few streets have names, and even these are rarely used in addresses. Even taxi drivers have trouble.
- Building numbers generally relate to the order of construction, not to position.
- In a Tokyo address such as 3-10-2 Akasaka (the district), Minato-ku (city ward), 3 is the subdivision or *chome* and 10-2 the building. "F" means floor; ground level is 1F. A map pinpointing the place and related landmarks is essential.

PUBLIC TRANSPORTATION

The subway
- Get a map of the system. Each line is identified by a color, used consistently on maps, signs, and sometimes on the trains too.
- At the station, find the row of ticket machines for that line. Price lists are displayed nearby. If you cannot find one, buy the lowest price ticket and pay any extra at your destination.
- Machines give change.

- Feed the ticket face up into the entry gate and collect it when the machine expels it. Make sure you keep it until the ride is over.
- Follow signs to the line and platform (track) you need, sometimes identified by the last station on the line, so check your map. Stand at the yellow markers, if any; wait to one side while passengers get off before boarding.
- At each stop, signs give the station's name and that of the next in Japanese and Roman script.
- At your destination, find an exit directory (a yellow board); note the number of the exit you want before going through the ticket gate. Otherwise you'll walk vast distances and probably get lost.
- Travel light, and at rush hour carry no bags at all. There are many stairs, and long walks to exits or when transferring between lines.

Trains
- Within Tokyo, the JR commuter and various private lines operate much the same as the subway.
- The JR Yamanote loop line links important central locations and can be quicker than the subway.
- Tickets are not interchangeable between JR, subway, and private lines.

Buses
- Public buses are slower and more confusing to use than the subway. Destinations, and information at stops, are usually marked only in Japanese characters.
- Make sure you know the route number, and have your destination written down in Japanese to show people when asking for help.
- On boarding, passengers take a numbered ticket. The fare is shown on an electronic display and paid on leaving the bus.

Where to get maps

- Larger hotels give out excellent city and subway maps; large stations supply subway maps.
- For both leaflets and maps, visit the Tourist Information Centers (TICs) run by JNTO at ⊠ **Narita Airport Terminal 2**, and in the city center at ⊠ **Basement of Tokyo International Forum, 3-5-1 Marunouchi, Chiyoda-ku** ☎ **3201–3331** ⊙ **Mon–Fri 9–5; Sat 9–12. Closed Sun and holidays.**

Discounts

- Subway (EIDAN and TOEI lines) and JR one-day tickets allow unlimited travel on their lines that day, but you will rarely justify the expense. A JR Orange Card, EIDAN Metro Card, and TOEI T Card can be used to obtain tickets until the stored value is spent. High denomination cards give a small discount.
- The Japan Rail Pass (for 7, 14, or 21 days unlimited travel on JR trains) is expensive, but can save money on long trips, for example by *shinkansen* ("bullet train") to Kyoto and back. An exchange order has to be purchased outside Japan, and exchanged for the pass itself at a main JR ticket counter. If you do this at Narita Airport on arrival you can use the pass to travel into the city.

Taxis

- The initial charge is high, ¥660 (and 30 percent more from 11PM–5AM) for the first 2km, and the fare then rises rapidly.
- A red light in the front window indicates that a taxi is available.
- Use the lefthand, curbside door; it opens and closes by remote control. Don't try to do it yourself.
- Drivers will rarely find anything but a big hotel, station or landmark from the address alone. To save time and money, show an area map with your destination marked.
- Pay only the fare on the meter. Tipping is not expected.

Driving

- Congestion, parking difficulties, and Japanese-only signs make it inadvisable for visitors to drive.
- Obtain an International Driving Permit before arrival in Japan, and bring your state license as well.
- Traffic keeps to the left. Driving standards have improved in recent years and are now quite good.

MEDIA & COMMUNICATIONS

Telephones

- Coin- and card-operated phones are prevalent. Local calls cost ¥10 per minute. ¥500 or ¥1,000 cards are sold at hotels, airports, station kiosks, and machines near phones.
- Make international direct-dial calls from gray and green phones with a gold front panel, card phones, or phones marked "international." Use only ¥100 coins, or cards. Several companies compete, each having its own international access code. Dial 001(for KDD), 0041 (ITJ) or 0061 (IDC), followed by the country code, area code (omit any initial 0), and number. The calling card codes of other international companies can also be used. MCI ☎ **0039–121 or 0066–55–121**; AT&T ☎ **0039–111 or 0066–55–111.**
- Direct dialing from hotel rooms is expensive.
- Dial 0051 for person-to-person and collect (reverse charge) calls, and 0057 (toll-free) for information.
- Mobile phones from other countries are not compatible with Japanese networks.

Fax

- Hotels and KDD offices can send faxes for you. Some hotels provide fax machines in the rooms, free or for an extra charge.

Post offices

- Hotel desks are the most convenient place to post letters and cards. They have stamps and are familiar with postal rates.
- Go to post offices only to send heavy packages or registered mail. Staff can read Roman script.
- Post offices open Mon–Fri 9–5.
- 24-hour post office: Tokyo International Post Office ✉ 2-3-3 Otemachi, Chiyoda-ku.

Newspapers

- There are four English-language translations of the main Japanese dailies: the *Japan Times*, *Daily Yomiuri*, *Mainichi Daily News*, and *Asahi Evening News*.
- The *International Herald Tribune*, *Financial Times*, and *Asian Wall Street Journal* are also available on the day of publication.
- Local English-language magazines (see below) are useful for listings of entertainment and restaurants.

Listings magazines

- The *Tokyo Journal* (monthly) has full listings of exhibitions, flea markets, services, and entertainment. However, restaurant, club, and bar reviews sometimes tend to be biased in favor of advertisers.
- *City Life News Tokyo* (monthly) and *Tokyo Weekender* (with Saturday's *Daily Yomiuri*) carry articles on the Tokyo scene.

International newsagents

- A full range of foreign magazines is stocked at news-stands in big hotels and major railway stations, and in large bookstores (➤ 76).

Radio

- FM radio stations broadcast Western and Japanese classical, popular, and rock music.
- The US armed services have a general information and entertainment AM radio station: Far East Network (FEN) 810 Hz.

Television

- The domestic TV channels have little to interest visitors, except perhaps the news and weather in simultaneous English translation (available at the push of a button on many sets), and the sport.
- Major hotels have satellite channels including news in English on CNN and BBC World.

EMERGENCIES

Sensible precautions

- Tokyo is the safest of the world's big cities to walk around. Even in the raunchier areas, such as Kabukicho, you need not be too apprehensive: when the locals drink too much, they are rarely aggressive. More problems are caused by drunken foreigners in the bars and discos of Roppongi.
- Use the hotel safes for storing large sums of money.

Lost property

- Trains: Teito (EIDAN) subway lines ☎ 3834–5577; TOEI lines: ☎ 3815–7229; JR trains ☎ 3231–1880 (Tokyo Station) ☎ 3841–8069 (Ueno Station)
- Taxis: ☎ 3648–0300
- Buses: ☎ 3818–5760

Medical treatment

- Standards are high, and so are costs. A good travel insurance policy should include comprehensive medical coverage.

- Your embassy can recommend hospitals with some doctors who speak English.

Medication

- For prescriptioin and non-prescription medication, when you need and English speaker: American Pharmacy ✚ K6 ✉ Hibiya Park Building 1-8-1 Yurakucho, Chiyoda-ku ☎ 3271–4034 🕐 Mon–Fri 9–7; Sat 11–6. Closed Sun and holidays 🚇 Ginza.

Emergency phone numbers

- Police ☎ 110
- Fire and Ambulance ☎ 119
- Emergency numbers are toll-free. On pay phones push the red button first.
- There are police boxes (*koban*) on many street corners and resident police in every little district. They usually speak only Japanese.

Embassies

- Australia ✉ 2-1-14 Mita, Minato-ku, Tokyo 108 ☎ 5232–4111
- Canada ✉ 7-3-38 Akasaka, Minato-ku, Tokyo 107 ☎ 3408–2101
- Germany ✉ 4-5-10 Minami-azabu, Minato-ku, 106 ☎ 3473–0151
- Netherlands ✉ 3-6-3 Shiba-koen, Minato-ku, 10 ☎ 5401–0411
- New Zealand ✉ 20-40 Kamiyama-cho, Shibuya-ku, Tokyo 150 ☎ 3467–2271
- UK ✉ 1 Ichiban-cho, Chiyoda-ku, Tokyo 102 ☎ 3265–5511
- USA ✉ 1-10-5 Akasaka, Minato-ku, Tokyo 107 ☎ 3224–5000

LANGUAGE

- Romanized versions of Japanese words are more or less phonetic, so say the words as written.
- Give all syllables equal weight, except: "u" at the end of a word, which is hardly sounded at all; "i" in the middle of a word, which is skipped over, as in mash'te for -mashite.
- E sounds like "eh" in ten; g is generally hard, as in go.
- Two adjoining consonants are sounded separately.
- A dash over a vowel lengthens the vowel sound.
- Family names are now usually written second.

Useful words & phrases

How do you do? Hajime-mashite?
Good morning Ohayo gozai-masu
Good afternoon Kon-nichi-wa
Good evening Konban-wa
Good night Oyasumi-nasai
Goodbye Sayo-nara
Mr, Mrs, Miss, Ms -san (suffix to family name, or given name of friends)
Thank you Domo/arigato
Don't mention it Do itashi-mashite
Excuse me, sorry Sumi-masen
Please (when offering) Dozo
Please (when asking) Kudasai
Yes Hai
Do you understand? Wakari-masu-ka?
Do you speak English? Eigo o hanashi-masu-ka?
I don't understand Japanese Nihon-go ga wakari-masen
How much is it? Ikura desu-ka?
Where is ...? ... wa doko desu-ka?
...train station ...eki
... hotel ... hoteru
left/right hidari/migi
north/south kita/minami
east/west higashi/nishi

Numbers

1	ichi	9	kyu (or ku)
2	ni	10	ju (or to)
3	san	11	ju-ichi
4	shi (or yon)	20	ni-ju
5	go	30	san-ju
6	roku	40	yon-ju
7	nana (or shichi)	100	hya-ku
8	hachi	1,000	sen

3 BEAUTIFUL PLACES:
KYOTO — AMA NO (VIEW) HASHIDATE
SHRINE
HIROSHIMA — ITSUKUSHIMA
SENDAI — MATSUSHIMA (ISLAND)

INDEX

Citypack
Tokyo

Copyright   © 1997 and 1999 by The Automobile Association
Maps copyright   © 1997 by The Automobile Association
Fold-out map: © RV Reise- und Verkehrsverlag Munich · Stuttgart
                   © Cartography: GeoData

Published in the United States by Fodor's Travel Publications, Inc.
Published in the United Kingdom by AA Publishing

Fodor's is a registered trademark of Fodor's Travel Publications, Inc.

ISBN 0–679–00246–4
Second Edition

FODOR'S CITYPACK TOKYO

AUTHOR *Martin Gostelow*
CARTOGRAPHY *The Automobile Association and RV Reise- und Verkehrsverlag*
COVER DESIGN *Fabrizio La Rocca, Allison Saltzman*
ORIGINAL COPY EDITOR *Susan Whimster*
REVISION VERIFIER *Martin Gostelow*
INDEXER *Marie Lorimer*
SECOND EDITION UPDATED BY *OutHouse Publishing Services*

Acknowledgments

The Automobile Association wishes to thank the following photographers, associations, and libraries for their assistance in the preparation of this book: M. GOSTELOW 5b, 16, 20, 35, 60, 63b; JAPANESE NATIONAL TOURIST ORGANISATION 62; NATIONAL MUSEUM OF MODERN ART 37b; OTA MEMORIAL MUSEUM OF ART 52; REX FEATURES LTD 9, 12; SPECTRUM COLOUR LIBRARY 1, 6, 7, 13a, 13b, 19, 21, 25a, 26, 28a, 30a, 30b, 36, 38a, 39, 40b, 41, 49b, 51a, 55, 63a; SUNTORY MUSEUM 53; TOKYO NATIONAL MUSEUM 25b; ZEFA PICTURES LTD 2, 5a, 87a. All remaining pictures are held in the Association's own library (AA PHOTO LIBRARY) and were taken by J. Holmes, with the exception of 27a, 46, 47, 49a, 59, which were taken by D. Corrance, and 29a, 29b, 37a, 42b, 87b, which were taken by R. T. Alford.

Special sales

Fodor's Travel Publications are available at special discounts for bulk purchases (100 copies or more) for sales promotions or premiums. Special editions, including personalized covers, excerpts of existing guides, and corporate imprints, can be created in large quantities for special needs. For more information contact your local bookseller or write to Special Marketing, Fodor's Travel Publications, 201 East 50th St., New York, NY 10022. Inquiries from Canada should be directed to your local Canadian bookseller or sent to Random House of Canada, Ltd., Marketing Department, 2775 Matheson Blvd. East, Mississauga, Ontario L4W 4P7.

Color separation by Daylight Colour Art Pte Ltd, Singapore
Manufactured by Dai Nippon Printing Co. (Hong Kong) Ltd
10 9 8 7 6 5 4 3 2 1

Titles in the Citypack series